DREAMS

VOLUME 2

VISIONS

&

DR. JOE IBOJIE

DREAMS
VOLUME 2
VISIONS

A Bible-Guided Meaning
to Your Dreams & Visions

CROSS HOUSE BOOKS
Christian Book Publishers
245 Midstocket Road
Aberdeen
AB15 5PH, UK

"The entrance of Your Word brings light."

Cover, Text Design and Typesetting by Jeffrey M. Hall, www.iongdw.com

ISBN: 978-0-9564008-1-9

For Worldwide Distribution, Printed in U.S.A.

2 3 4 5 6 7 8 / 22 21 20 19 18

To order products by Dr. Joe Ibojie & other Cross House Books, contact sales@crosshousebooks.co.uk.

Other correspondence: info@crosshousebooks.co.uk.
Visit www.crosshousebooks.co.uk.

DEDICATION

I DEDICATE THIS BOOK to my wife, Cynthia.

The Bible says, *"He who finds a wife finds a good thing"* (Prov. 18:22). This is my testimony.

Often you have had to abandon your personal pursuits to further our ministry goals. You crossed my t's and dotted my i's. You are a silent but selfless worker in the Body of Christ.

Surely the honor and blessing of a wife who covers her husband's nakedness and enhances his gifting will rest upon you abundantly. Thank you for who you are.

You have all of my love, Oyin (Honey).

Your husband,

Joe

WHAT OTHERS
ARE SAYING

The Bible is full of dreams and full of visions—more than 200 recorded instances combined! God uses dreams and visions to communicate to prophets, kings, wise men, and apostles, and are mentioned throughout Scripture from Genesis to Revelation. God uses dreams and visions in the Bible, and He continues to use them to communicate with us today. This being the case, it would seem that there should be vast volumes printed on the topic; however, it is only in recent years that Christian authors have paid any real attention to the subjects of dreams and visions.

Joe Ibojie has been at the forefront (especially concerning dreams) in bringing light to what most Christians have always suspected—God speaks to us in our dreams. I found this book to be a delight. Most books concerning dreams and their interpretation are mere introductions. But *Dreams and Visions Volume 2* takes the reader deeper into understanding and it does so with a hefty dose of Scripture on every page with a light seasoning of personal experience! It is clear that this book has been written with a wonderful mixture of diligent research and practical experience.

What I appreciate most about Joe's approach is how he takes a subject most consider to be entirely subjective in nature (dreams and visions) and then grounds it in Scripture, giving loads of practical advice about how to remember dreams and how to interpret them. I really can't recommend this book highly enough.

If you dream, which I am certain that you do, then this book is for you.

—Pastor Phil Sanderson
Third Day Church
Aberdeen, Scotland, UK

Dr. Joe Ibojie is a man of God with outstanding character. He is a foremost authority in biblical studies, Bible symbolism, and interpretation of dreams and visions. He carries a unique and powerful anointing for divine revelation and wisdom that has blessed countless people worldwide.

This man of God has been a blessing to my ministry. If you truly want to know a man, go to his home base. I have ministered with Joe Ibojie on several occasions at his home church, The Father's House, in Aberdeen, Scotland, and like the Queen of Sheba once said, I could say, *"half was not told me."* The Father's House congregation is vibrant and exudes genuine Christian effervescence that is rare these days. Indeed, I consider him a close and trusted friend.

This new addition to his exciting and inspirational writings, *Dreams and Visions Volume 2,* is a phenomenal book that renews the faith and passion of believers to press forward in expectation of God's will being manifested. It also instructs believers about the keys to hearing God in dreams and visions and so helps them to discover and unlock God's divine authority in their lives. This book is sure to become a timeless masterpiece, one that will transcend generations and teach future believers how to hear the voice of God in the night season.

—Mario Maxwell, President
Mario Maxwell International Ministries
Oklahoma City, Oklahoma, USA

PRAISE FOR
DREAMS AND VISIONS VOLUME 1

There are some people raised to speak to the nations of the world, who do not realize they have insight that only God gives. I believe Dr. Joe Ibojie is one of the voices that God has raised up to speak and give revelation and insight concerning our destiny.

This book, *Dreams and Visions: How to receive, interpret and apply your dreams* will bless you and change your life as it helps you to gain insightful knowledge of what God is speaking to you in dreams and visions. As you read this book, the eyes of your understanding will be enlightened and God will open up the doors that have been closed in your life.

I highly recommend this book to every preacher, every Christian and any one who has ever had a dream or vision and who really wants to understand their spiritual encounters with God.

—Bishop John Francis
Senior Pastor, Rauch Ministries
London, UK

Dreams and Visions stands tall among other books you might read on the subject of dreams and visions. It teaches the reader to understand and appreciate the voice of God in the night season of life through practical principles inherent in the Word of God. The author, Joe Ibojie, ministered in Cali, Colombia, and profoundly imparted to the Colombian Christians. The anointing of God was clearly evident in Joe's ministry as he taught and ministered with deep and dynamic revelation to church leaders in Colombia. I recommend this book to all believers, young and old, including pastors and church leaders. This book will create a new hunger in the Body of Christ and will cause them to listen to the voice of God and be guided by the Holy Spirit in a completely new way.

—Apostle Randy MacMillan
Founder of Mission South America
Norfolk, Virginia, USA

This book and its Bible-based dictionary are a mighty tool in the hand of those in the Body of Christ who are seeking to recognize the voice of God in their life. God has blessed Dr. Ibojie not only with a powerful anointing and gift himself, but also with the grace to help others unlock the inner potential within themselves through powerful keys of wisdom and insight. This book is a treasure chest filled with God's revelation and hidden mysteries that have been waiting to be uncovered since before the foundation of the earth. *Dreams and Visions* shall bless, strengthen, and guide any believer in search of the purpose, promise, and destiny of God for their lives. Thank God for this Christ-centered, Bible-based message that will restore the awareness that God continually longs to communicate His love, desires, and will to His children. *"He who watches over Israel will never slumber nor sleep"* (Ps. 121:4). While you are sleeping, He is still speaking. Let he who has an ear (and the desire to hear) listen to what the Spirit is saying to the Church.

—Bishop Ron Scott Jr.
President, Kingdom Coalition International
Hagerstown, Maryland, USA

This is a comprehensive study of the reality of spiritual dreaming. The significance of the prophetic language of dreams and how God's eternal purpose is expressed in our dreams is well-established. Dr. Ibojie has studied the Scripture and uses biblical keys to unlock understanding into this supernatural area of divine communication. He is a meticulous teacher of the Word of God and a wise master builder, and his explanation of the interpretation of dreams is a foundational teaching that will greatly assist the believer in understanding the significance of dreams, without moving into error.

This study is balanced, well-written, and very motivational. It will be a blessing to the Body of Christ and is a must-read for all teachers of prophecy, elders of the congregation, and students of dreams.

—Emmanuel Ziga
President, Grace for All Nations Ministries International
Seattle, Washington, USA

The prophet Joel declares that "in the last days" the Holy Spirit's outpouring will include an increase in dreams and visions as a form of prophetic gifting. How many of us have had dreams and visions without realizing that God may be speaking to us in parables? It stands to godly reason that if the Lord is indeed speaking to us while we sleep, then He will also give the gift of interpretation so that we may understand what He is saying. In *Dreams and Visions*, Joe Ibojie presents sound scriptural principles and practical advice that can help us to this end. As Joe repeatedly makes clear, such understanding is not formula-based, nor is it human reason, but "interpretation is of the Lord." Therefore, we must diligently seek Him.

Joe Ibojie is a medical doctor who is also an ordained minister of the gospel. He has an effective prophetic ministry with a Daniel-type anointing in the interpretation of dreams. That this book is clearly rooted in the Word of God is evidenced by his encyclopedic knowledge and Scripture use. I am sure many readers will gain much spiritual benefit from a careful reading of this book.

—Gordon Shewan
Senior Pastor, All Nations Christian Fellowship
Aberdeen, Scotland, UK

Father God desires to speak to His people. The Lord is doing much of His communication in visions and dreams, but it has been difficult for many to determine what is from God and what is not. The Lord has given Dr. Joe a divine insight into the way He speaks to us through such heavenly encounters. This book is a practical guide that helps answer many questions, including God's purposes and types of dreams and visions and what they typically mean. There is also a wonderful chapter on how to hear the voice of God. We have found *Dreams and Visions* to be the best book we have read in regard to dreams and visions. Our prayers are for this book to be a blessing to many hearing the call of destiny from God as it's expressed to us in visions and dreams.

—Robert and Joyce Ricciardelli
Directors, Visionary Advancement Strategies
Seattle, Washington, USA
www.vision2advance.com

I have been privileged to minister with Joe on a frequent basis. However, I am more privileged to know him not just as a person with Daniel-type anointing or as a prophetic voice (although he is frequently both of these to me), but as one of my closest friends. A true servant of God, Joe is a man with a passion to see God's kingdom extend wherever he goes and to whomever he meets. Writing this book is simply an extension of that passion and it has come out of years of experience. He has worked it out on a practical level and seen people transformed and set free to a life of liberty and purpose in the Holy

Spirit. Others have been built up, encouraged, and edified because they gained a clearer understanding of God's purposes and plans in their lives through a godly and, I believe, biblical interpretation of their dreams.

Dreams and Visions is a book to be revisited time and again. It corrects much of the flaky teaching about dreams that is often propagated and seeks to anchor everything in the truth and steadfast surety of Scripture. This is a book that every prophetic person in the Church should have and should study, weigh, and test it against Scripture. This book should be placed not on a shelf, but on a nightstand!

—Pastor Phil Sanderson
All Nations Christian Fellowship
Aberdeen, Scotland, UK

Dr. Joe Ibojie is a true man of God who walks in real integrity and ministers under the anointing and inspiration of the Holy Spirit. Accurate prophetic revelation flows as Dr. Joe interprets dreams. I see this book as a manual to equip and inspire you in this area. The timing is just right for the release of this book, which is sure to unlock incredible truths that lie within your dreams and visions. As you read, God will open up your understanding on this little-heard truth and reveal a whole new avenue of hearing God's voice. Highly recommended as a must-read for every dreamer!

—Duncan Wyllie
Senior Pastor, Kairo Christian Outreach Center
Peterhead, Scotland, UK

Dreams and Visions is a wonderful tool to help train and equip today's believers in the revelatory realm of dreams, as well as their interpretation and application. Dr. Joe Ibojie presents a vibrant book that is both inspiring and challenging.

—Catherine Brown
Founder, Gatekeepers Prayer & Mission
Glasgow, Scotland, UK
www.gatekeepers.org.uk
www.millionhoursofpraise.com

I have worked closely with Dr. Joe Ibojie as a member of the pastoral team of All Nations Church and the Greater Church in Aberdeenshire. It has been my privilege to have had access to this book's genius and to monitor its progress from conception to completion. Joe has an extraordinary understanding of the meaning of dreams and the ministry of angels. He is a man of unusual gifting, passion, and tenderness, and his writing portrays the gracious nature of his character. The impact of his insights has had a profound effect on me. On numerous occasions, I have observed firsthand the liberty, joy, and peace that many individuals have received through Joe's ability to interpret, with certainty, the mysteries of their dreams. He is becoming a popular speaker in church conferences as his gifting is becoming better known and sought after by Christians. I am persuaded that *Dreams and Visions* will equip and enable many readers to develop a similar understanding of their own dreams. This book should generate a persuasion throughout the Church of the significance of dreams and their place in the myriad ways that God reveals Himself to mankind.

—Reverend Hector Mackenzie
Bible Teacher, Director, Christian Solidarity Worldwide
All Nation Christian Fellowship
Aberdeen, Scotland, UK

I've always had very vivid dreams, and it's only now that I've started to unravel them with the help of *Dreams and Visions*. For the first time during prayer, I've started to receive pictures as well. This book has truly blessed me immensely.

—Jess Howells
Editor
Kent, England, UK

I have always been skeptical about this "dream thing," but there is a certain balance in this book that brings about an enjoyment in dream interpretation. I am proud of this hard work for the Kingdom. I have enjoyed and learned from reading this book by my beloved son Dr. Joe Ibojie. If the Bible talks about it, we cannot afford to be silent. Thanks for this insight!

—Bishop Fred Addo
International Praise Cathedral Kaduna, Nigeria

TABLE OF CONTENTS

FOREWORD

JOE HAS WRITTEN *Dreams and Visions Volume 2* with remarkable clarity and brings further illumination to the puzzles that surround the ancient subject of dreams and visions and their value and relevance in the contemporary world.

I am honored and privileged to write the Foreword to *Dreams and Visions Volume 2.* I am honored because it is truly great book that will inspire and encourage the Body of Christ and all of the dreamers who are far too many to count. Privileged because I co-pastor with Dr. Joe Ibojie, my husband, and the author of this book, a great man of God—a true servant of God.

When the first book on dreams and visions was published a few years ago, it soon became clear that it was a book for everyone—anyone who has ever had a dream. For most of us, it was a significant paradigm shift toward the eternal truth of God on this fascinating subject. Thousands of people worldwide have been blessed by the insights shared in *Dreams and Visions Volume 1,* and now the book has many foreign translations to its credit.

I remember vividly that when Joe proceeded to have the first volume published, he confided to me that "the ink was still flowing," but that the Lord asked him to proceed to publication. Yes indeed, our times are in God's hands, and He makes everything beautiful in its own time. God is true to His promises, *the ink never dried up, the oil never ceased, and the water kept flowing!*

I have watched over the years as my husband labored ceaselessly to ensure that he ministered to the saints of God only from the abundance of richness of his relationship with God. Perhaps my audacity to write this Foreword also stems from the many lonely nights I have waited for him to come to the bedroom. In this waiting, I have had to be comforted and encouraged by God Himself. I have been truly blessed indeed!

The second volume of *Dreams and Visions* is now in your hands. It will bring clearer understanding to your dreams and visions—it is a worthy sequel to the success of *Dreams and Visions Volume 1*. This book is packaged in a reader-friendly way and will teach you: how to know when God speaks into your spirit; how to remember your dreams; and explain the dreams mentioned in the Scriptures in a new, fresh, and in-depth way.

You will be blessed!

Pastor Cynthia Ibojie
Senior Pastor
The Father's House
Aberdeen, Scotland, UK

INTRODUCTION

THE BIBLE SPEAKS OF how God used dreams and visions at critical points to guide and direct the lives of people and nations in those days. In the Old and New Testaments dreams carried special significance and are often one of the ways by which God makes known His will to man. For instance, Joseph, of the coat of many colors, had dreams of his rulership many years before it was fulfilled; Abimelech, the Philistine king, was warned in a dream that Sarah was the wife of Abraham; Joseph, the earthly father of Jesus was encouraged to marry Mary and later he was warned to take Mary and Jesus to Egypt when Jesus' life was in peril. Therefore, one can say of the past, *"God, who at various times, and in various ways spoke in time past to the fathers by the prophets"* (Heb. 1:1 NKJV), in dreams (see Dan. 7:1-14) in visions (see Ezek. 8:4), by angels (see Zech. 19:9), by the burning bush (see Exod. 3:4), and by direct audible voice (see Gen. 12:1).

Concerning the present age, God also says, *"If there is a prophet among you, I, the Lord, make Myself known to him in a vision; I speak to him in a dream"* (Num. 12:6).

And speaking of the future, God says, *"It shall come to pass in the last days, says God, that I will pour out of My Spirit on all flesh; your sons and daughters shall prophesy, your young men shall see visions and your old men shall dream dreams"* (Acts 2:17).

Clearly then, God spoke in time past through dreams and visions, and at present He continues to speak through them and will speak through them in the future. On our part we can no longer afford to be silent about them. Everyone dreams. A great percentage of the members of every local church receives and ponders on dreams and visions on an everyday basis. Within any local congregation of Christians is a thriving community of people desperate to find meaning for their nightly encounters. It is time to choose to acknowledge their existence and do something to bring the light of God into the situation. The alternative is to sit back and allow innocent people to drift into darkness and into the hand of the prince of the darkness.

The more the church distances itself from this valuable means of divine communication, the more erroneous and frustrating interpretation drives honest Christians into spiritual bondage. The world is continually being inundated by rapidly expanding occult literature and misinformation on the subject of dreams and visions. Non-Christian literature is full of deception, profiteering, and confusion on this subject. We can no longer sit back and assume we can do nothing. Man's greatest asset on earth is not only his ability to hear from God but also his ability to both hear and understand what God says. Dreams and visions are sure ways for God to direct the steps of the righteous man and will remain ways to bring the agenda of Heaven to the earth.

Modern lies about dreams and superstitious attitudes regarding dreams are mostly due to the fact that they are available to all, Christians and non-Christians alike. Without the Holy Spirit, the majority of non-believers treat dreams and visions as omens and seek to utilize them outside God's purposes. Such practices amount to using godly principles in an ungodly way and are a form of divination. This has dented the image of dreams and visions within the Christian community. We need to carefully restore this valuable means of divine communication using biblical methods.

DREAMS AND VISIONS ARE IMPORTANT

Dreams are important and continue to be relevant to the times we live in—they are far from being obsolete. Dreams are ancient biblical forms of divine communication that need prayerful study and careful application in our present-day living. If God trusted the marriage of Mary and Joseph, the earthly parents of Jesus, and the protection of baby Jesus to a few short and vivid dreams, we ought to take the subject of dreams more seriously. It was in a vision that apostle Paul received the

Macedonian call and perhaps that was how the gospel got into Europe at the time it did. Abraham's covenant was consummated in a vision and a dream. Most of the major prophets in biblical days were either called in visions or in dreams; Ezekiel, Isaiah, and the apostle Paul received their call to ministry in dreams or in visions. The entire Book of Revelation is comprised of the visions that apostle John received while living on the Island of Patmos. King Abimelech would have lost his life and brought a severe curse upon his people if he had disregarded the advice given to him in a dream. Jacob was given the strategy for economic breakthrough in a dream when he suffered injustice by the hands of his uncle Laban. From Genesis to Revelation and up to our modern times, the importance and relevance of dreams and visions in individuals and the collective destiny of the world cannot be ignored.

In my first book on dreams and visions, there was special emphasis on exploring the fundamentals of dreams and vision as they relate to our everyday living. In this second volume, the teaching is slanted to emphasize how to gain clearer understanding of our dreams and visions in a new, in-depth and user-friendly way. This is important, if we are to avail ourselves of the valuable wisdom keys inherent in dreams and visions that we receive.

The Bible says, *"In all your getting, get understanding"* (Prov. 4:7b). From the foundation of time, the bone of contention underscoring the war and the things of the spirit realm nearly always surrounds the battle over gaining proper understanding and knowledge. No wonder God Himself lamented that *"My people are destroyed for lack of knowledge"* (Hosea 4:6) and again that the truth you know will set you free. In the Book of Daniel, we are given a glimpse of this struggle in action and of the continuous battle over gaining proper understanding of things happening in the heavens.

The Bible records the story of how an evil principality ruling over Persia withheld the angelic messenger sent to bring understanding to the prophet Daniel. In this case the angelic messenger was delayed for twenty-one days in the heavenly realm. The devil, through the evil prince of Persia, was desperate to withhold understanding from the Jewish captives in Babylon and by so doing to delay their return to their homeland (see Dan. 10:12-14). Truly, *"Understanding is the wellspring of life to him who has it"* (Prov. 16:22). This second volume on dreams and visions is pivoted on getting clear understanding of dreams and visions.

WE NEED TO UNDERSTAND OUR DREAMS AND VISIONS

In the last days, not only will "old men" dream dreams and "young men" see visions, but also there will be a corresponding release of the spirit of understanding from the very throne of God. God will pour out divine illumination for the understanding of these dreams and visions. Illuminating insights emanating from the very doors of the third heaven will come upon the earth to bring explanation to the mysteries or hidden things of God like never before. The administration of this grace for divine understanding of the mysteries of God will come upon many servants of God in a new and fresh way. This is a particular grace to understand the dark speeches of God, riddles, and sticky problems of life. (Dark speeches are the things of God that have hidden meaning and unless unfolded by God, the human mind on its own cannot grasp the true and complete perspective.) It is therefore important to recognize when the Spirit of God brings simplicity to the things that have been regarded as complex over the ages. Ours is a privileged generation, but we must make the best of the grace granted us.

On our part, it is time to make conscious efforts to leave shallow understanding of our dreams and visions and move into their proper understanding. In this way, we can maximize the benefits of the divine wisdom keys inherent in the dreams that we receive. Imagine, for instance, if Joseph (of coat of many colors), simply told Pharaoh that the meaning of his dream was that something bad was going to happen after a period of a good harvest. (See Genesis 41.) You know, he would have been right, but it would have fallen short of the wisdom keys God intended for the king to have. Yet as I travel around the world I see the prevalence of that type of shallow and partial interpretation everywhere I go. It has got to be a lot more than that!

It is for this course that this book is dedicated.

PART I

DREAMS

Chapter 1

Understanding Yourself and Your Dreams

PERHAPS THIS CHAPTER is not so much of an issue for those who are already operating from an established method of communication with God. But for the majority of dreamers at the local church level, the problem of judging by the flesh and constant intrusions from the human mind remain an incessant difficulty. I have put together issues that may be challenging to budding dreamers and discuss how they may recognize and disentangle themselves from these humanistic tendencies that we all face in a world system tending toward absolute humanism. The power to overcome these tendencies is vital if the dreamer is to hear God's voice clearly and become a vessel fit for the Master's use.

God speaks in a variety of ways: through the Bible; in dreams; in visions; experiencing trances, visitations, translations; and through His audible voice or other peoples' voices. No matter how we hear His voice, we need to confirm that what we have heard is from God. Many voices exist in the spirit world, but God's voice will be recognizable if our spirit bears witness to it, it lines up with Scripture, and if it speaks of His love.

Hearing from God must begin where we are, gradually and progressing forward toward more mature and often more complex forms of divine communication. So for most people, divine inspiration may occur as a mere impression, or perhaps a prompting such as a flash of ideas, a picture, a birthing in the spirit, or even a knowing of conviction. However, we require maturity to distinguish what is of God and what is not. Our only security in this process lies in walking in love and in realizing that we should come to God just as little children come to a natural father—with transparent innocence and simplicity. In other words, stepping out in faith and humility will move us from the stage of impression into greater spiritual encounters with divinity.

Maturity in the spirit only comes through a process of consistent use of our spiritual senses. This principle applies in the natural as well as in the spiritual. As explained in Hebrews 5:14, mature believers are those who—through consistent exercise of their spiritual senses—can discriminate between sound and unsound doctrines and between wholesome and unwholesome conduct. The only way to grow in God is to learn to walk with God. If we are afraid of misunderstanding what God says, then we will never master the art of hearing God and walking in His obedience. We need to approach the issue with reverence and realize that no man shall prevail by his strength.

> *But solid food belongs to those who are of full age, that is, those who by reason of use have their senses exercised to discern both good and evil* (Hebrews 5:14).

DISCERNING VOICES IN THE SPIRIT REALM

The Voice of God

The first voice Adam heard was the voice of God: *"And the Lord God commanded the man, 'You are free to eat from any tree in the garden; but you must not eat from the tree of the knowledge of good and evil, for when you eat of it you will surely die'"* (Gen. 2:16-17).

There are four ways that people hear the voice of God.

1. Some are hearers—their gift is predominantly in the ability to hear what God is saying.

2. Some are feelers—they feel what God wants to communicate, such as feeling pain in the part of the body where God wants to heal someone.

3. Some are seers—they are gifted in the ability to see pictures, flashes of pictures, and dreams and visions on a constant basis.

4. Others are spiritually sensitive enough to discern what God is saying by the spirit of discernment.

No matter how you hear the voice of God, you will need to confirm that it is God. There are many voices in the spirit world, but the voice of God is easily recognizable if the message is subjected to the following checks. Does the message:

- Lead you to greater intimacy with God?
- Lead to expression of love? (For God is love.)
- Put God's benefit and the interest of others before personal benefit?
- Lead to greater manifestations of Christ-likeness?
- Lead to more humility? Or does it appeal to the ego?
- Generate more joy, peace, and righteousness? (The Kingdom of God is love, peace, and righteousness in the Holy Spirit.)
- Lead to greater dependence on God?
- Line up with the written Word of God?

If it does, it's more than likely a message from God.

The Voice of Other People

The next voice that Adam heard was that of Eve. The voice of Eve was the first human voice heard by Adam.

The Lord God said, "It is not good for the man to be alone. I will make a helper suitable for him" (Genesis 2:18).

So the man gave names to all the livestock, the birds of the air and all the beasts of the field. But for Adam no suitable helper was found. So the Lord God caused the man to fall into a deep sleep; and while he was sleeping, He took one of the man's ribs and closed up the place with flesh. Then the Lord God made a woman from the rib He had taken out of the man, and He brought her to the man. The man said, "This is now bone of my bones and flesh of my flesh; she shall be called 'woman,' for she was taken out of man." For this reason a man will leave his father and mother and be united to his wife, and they will become one flesh. The man and his wife were both naked, and they felt no shame" (Genesis 2:20-25).

What you hear from other people can bias your mind. Jesus Christ said we should be careful what we listen to. What you hear can interfere with the way you process the things you receive spiritually or naturally. Many people today are not able to receive from very anointed messengers because of what they heard about the messenger.

The Voice of the Devil and His Agents

The next voice that mankind heard (apart from the voice of God and other people) was the voice of satan.

Now the serpent was more crafty than any of the wild animals the Lord God had made. He said to the woman, "Did God really say, 'You must not eat from any tree in the garden'?" The woman said to the serpent, "We may eat fruit from the trees in the garden, but God did say, 'You must not eat fruit from the tree that is in the middle of the garden, and you must not touch it, or you will die.'" "You will not surely die," the serpent said to the woman. "For God knows that when you eat of it your eyes will be opened, and you will be like God, knowing good and evil" (Genesis 3:1-5).

We can hear the voice of satan in a variety of ways. Satan can speak to man in an audible voice, he can put ideas into the human mind, and he can cause bewitchment. Apostle Paul asked the Galatians, *"O foolish Galatians! Who has bewitched you that you should not obey the truth"* (Gal. 3:1).

Satan can cause confusion or blindness to the human mind:

*The evening meal was being served, and **the devil had already prompted** Judas Iscariot, son of Simon, to betray Jesus* (John 13:2).

***The god of this age has blinded the minds of unbelievers,** so that they cannot see the light of the gospel of the glory of Christ, who is the image of God* (2 Corinthians 4:4).

***Satan rose up against Israel and incited** David to take a census of Israel* (1 Chronicles 21:1).

Satan's favorite method is destabilizing a person, and then infiltrating him or her in order to cause confusion. If he succeeds in this, then he gradually takes over the person's reasoning faculty.

The Voice of the Flesh or Self

The next voice that man heard was the voice of the activated soul, the voice of the flesh. This is also the echo of our desires good or bad, including the voice of human logic or the voice of intellectualism. It is also the voice of our bodily desires, covetousness, the lust of the eyes, the pride of life, and the lust of the flesh.

But the Lord God called to the man, "Where are you?" He answered, "I heard you in the garden, and I was afraid because I was naked; so I hid." And he said, "Who told you that you were naked? Have you eaten from the tree from which I commanded you not to eat?" The man said, "The woman you put here with me—she gave me some fruit from the tree, and I ate it." Then the Lord God said to the woman, "What is this you have done?" The woman said, "The serpent deceived me, and I ate" (Genesis 3:9-13).

God asked Adam and Eve, who told them that they were naked. It was self-realization that made them aware of their nakedness. This is the voice of the flesh or the voice of the human mind. Notice that before this point the Bible says they were naked but they were not ashamed (see Gen. 2:25).

The voice of the flesh is important because unless we deliberately put off the voice of the mind, we cannot hear meaningfully from God. Our mind, emotions, and desires can play out in our dreams and visions or any other form of revelation. The way we use our natural and spiritual senses can influence how we hear from God, therefore it is important that we know how these senses operate.

PREPARING TO HEAR AND DISCERN SPIRIT-REALM VOICES

Strengthen your spirit.

We need to strengthen the human spirit to receive revelation. In the words of apostle Paul, the man is made up of the spirit, soul, and body:

> *May God Himself, the God of peace, sanctify you through and through. May your whole spirit, soul and body be kept blameless at the coming of our Lord Jesus Christ* (1 Thessalonians 5:23).

You strengthen your spirit by crucifying the flesh, studying the Word of God and dwelling in the presence of God. Spiritual senses outlive the natural senses. The story of Lazarus and the rich man illustrates this.

> *There was a rich man who was dressed in purple and fine linen and lived in luxury every day. At his gate was laid a beggar named Lazarus, covered with sores and longing to eat what fell from the rich man's table. Even the dogs came and licked his sores. The time came when the beggar died and the angels carried him to Abraham's side. The rich man also died and was buried. In hell, where he was in torment, he looked up and saw Abraham far away, with Lazarus by his side. So he called to him, 'Father Abraham, have pity on me and send Lazarus to dip the tip of his finger in water and cool my tongue, because I am in agony in this fire.' But Abraham replied, 'Son, remember that in your lifetime you received your good things, while Lazarus received bad things, but now he is comforted here and you are in agony. And besides all this, between us and you a great chasm has been fixed, so that those who want to go from here to you cannot, nor can anyone cross over from there to us.' He answered, 'Then I beg you, father, send*

Lazarus to my father's house, for I have five brothers. Let him warn them, so that they will not also come to this place of torment.' Abraham replied, 'They have Moses and the Prophets; let them listen to them.' No, father Abraham,' he said, 'but if someone from the dead goes to them, they will repent.' He said to him, 'If they do not listen to Moses and the Prophets, they will not be convinced even if someone rises from the dead' (Luke 16:19-31).

The strength of our spirit man determines the level of our effectiveness in spiritual things. I define the strength of the human spirit as the capacity of the human spirit to bear witness with the Spirit of God. It also means the capacity for responding to the prompting of the Holy Spirit and for participation in the happenings in the heavenly realm. Strengthening your spirit entails all that is necessary to bring your spirit man into a position of effectiveness and a place of minimal interference from the body and the soul.

The human spirit consists of three functional components: 1. Divine wisdom (see James 3:17), which is life application of the Word of God; 2. Sanctified conscience (see Heb. 9:14), which is the laying aside of personal agendas (Rom. 12:10); and 3. Communion with God (see Ps. 91:1 and Rom. 8:16), which is spending quality time with God. Purposeful application of these three components strengthens the human spirit.

Sharpen Your Spiritual Senses

Spiritual senses are the senses that are operative from the spirit of man, also known as the senses of our faith, because the spirit man operates by faith. Whereas natural senses are limited in the dimensions of time, space, height, and depth, there are no limitations with perception, using the pure and unpolluted spiritual senses.

The superiority of the spiritual senses is because they are capable of operating in the spiritual and in the natural realms, but the natural senses can only operate in the natural. By the spiritual senses, Adam and Eve were, therefore, able to live in the Garden of Eden, even though their natural senses were not yet "opened." They were dependent solely on their spiritual senses until the point when the Bible records that "the eyes of both of them were opened, and they realized they were naked" (Gen. 3:7). This was the point from which the natural eyes became active consequent to eating from the tree of knowledge of good and evil. From that point, the soul of man continues to increase, tending to encapsulate the spiritual senses.

The Bible teaches us that spiritual exercise is more valuable than physical exercises:

> *Don't waste time arguing over foolish ideas and silly myths and legends. Spend your time and energy in the exercise of keeping spiritually fit. Bodily exercise is all right,* **but spiritual exercise is much more important** *and is a tonic for all you do. So exercise yourself spiritually, and practice being a better Christian because that will help you not only now in this life, but in the next life too* (1 Timothy 4:7-8 TLB).

Strengthen Your Inner Spirit (Man)

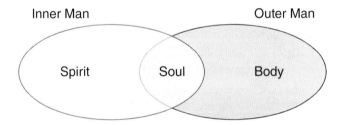

In the diagram, the soul is the non-tangible and immaterial part of man. The soul of man is also the relational part of man. When the spirit is strong, it dominates the soul, and when the body is strong, it dominates the soul. Therefore, the soul can go either way, whichever is the stronger, spirit or body, controls the soul.

The soul and the body together represent *the outer man*. On the other hand, the soul and the human spirit together, constitute *the inner man*. A controlled soul means the emotions are controlled, the mind is renewed and submitted to God, and the will is yielded to God.

The strength of the inner man is determined by the strength of the spirit supported by the strength of the soul. Note that it is possible to have a weak soul and yet be strong in the spirit. For instance, Samson was strong spiritually, being anointed from the womb of his mother as a Nazarite, but he manifested weakness in his soul at the same time. This caused him to fall. John the Baptist had a strong inner man.

In his case, he was also anointed from the womb of his mother but he ruled over his soul. This is why apostle Paul prayed that the Ephesians should be strengthened in their inner man:

> *For this reason I kneel before the Father, from whom His whole family in heaven and on earth derives its name. I pray that out of His glorious riches **He may strengthen you with power through His Spirit in your inner being**, so that Christ may dwell in your hearts through faith. And I pray that you, being rooted and established in love, may have power, together with all the saints, to grasp how wide and long and high and deep is the love of Christ, and to know this love that surpasses knowledge—that you may be filled to the measure of all the fullness of God* (Ephesians 3:14-19).

The eternal Word of God is foundational to the outworking of any ministry. The Word of God strengthens the human spirit. Before both Ezekiel and apostle John began their ministries, God made them symbolically eat the scroll, the Word of God. For prophet Samuel, his word came to the whole of Israel after the Word of God came to him.

Other things we need to do to enhance our ability to hear from God is to "put off your old self." This is how the Living Bible translates Ephesians 4:20-22: *"But that is not the way Christ taught you! If you have really heard His voice and learned from Him the truths concerning Himself, then throw off your old evil nature—the old you that was a partner in your evil ways—rotten through and through, full of lust and shame."*

The outer man is the sum total of our outward interactive front with the fallen world before gaining the true knowledge of the Triune God. The outer man is the body and the soul not under the rule of the spirit. The body and the soul tend to be in mutiny to the Spirit of God. That is why the Bible says they are contrary one to another (see Gal. 5:17). The soul is the relational component of man. On the one hand, if the body is strong, it dominates the soul and results in carnality. On the other hand, if the spirit is strong, it dominates the soul and enhances spirituality.

The outer man must progressively give way to the inner man as the Bible says:

Therefore we do not lose heart. Even though our outward [outer] *man is perishing, yet the inward* [inner] *man is being renewed day by day* (2 Corinthians 4:16).

Your beauty should not come from outward adornment, such as braided hair and the wearing of gold jewellery and fine clothes. Instead, it should be that of your inner self, the unfading beauty of a gentle and quiet spirit, which is of great worth in God's sight (1 Peter 3:3-4).

The "old man" refers to the person's pre-Christian ways of life. A new self in Christ Jesus should replace the *old man*. It is therefore the totality of life before coming to a true knowledge of God:

You were taught, with regard to your former way of life, to put off your old self, which is being corrupted by its deceitful desires; to be made new in the attitude of your minds; and to put on the new self, created to be like God in true righteousness and holiness (Ephesians 4:22-24).

In the *old man*, the corrupt, depraved and fallen nature of man rules. Such a person is not borne of the incorruptible seed of the eternal Word of God. The *old man* is the summation of the fallen state of humanity and of man's rebellion. The only possible work of the *old man* leads to defeat, failure, sin, and ultimately death. Unless the person repents, there is no alternative in his life but to remain a prisoner of his sinful nature. The Bible says that the works of the flesh include:

The acts of the sinful nature are obvious: sexual immorality, impurity and debauchery; idolatry and witchcraft; hatred, discord, jealousy, fits of rage, selfish ambition, dissensions, factions (Galatians 5:19-20).

Therefore God gave them over in the sinful desires of their hearts to sexual impurity for the degrading of their bodies with one another. They exchanged the truth of God for a lie, and worshiped and served created things rather than the Creator—who is forever praised.

Amen. Because of this, God gave them over to shameful lusts. Even their women exchanged natural relations for unnatural ones. In the same way the men also abandoned natural relations with women and were inflamed with lust for one another. Men committed indecent acts with other men, and received in themselves the due penalty for their perversion. Furthermore, since they did not think it worthwhile to retain the knowledge of God, he gave them over to a depraved mind, to do what ought not to be done. They have become filled with every kind of wickedness, evil, greed and depravity. They are full of envy, murder, strife, deceit and malice. They are gossips, slanderers, God-haters, insolent, arrogant and boastful; they invent ways of doing evil; they disobey their parents; they are senseless, faithless, heartless, and ruthless. Although they know God's righteous decree that those who do such things deserve death, they not only continue to do these very things but also approve of those who practise them (Romans 1:24-32).

Flesh or carnality is the combination of the body and the soul without the rule of the Spirit of God, and must be crucified, *"Those who belong to Christ Jesus have crucified the sinful nature with its passions and desires"* (Gal. 5:24).

Put on Your New Self

I like the Living Bible translation of Ephesians 4:23-24: *"Now your attitudes and thoughts must all be constantly changing for the better. Yes, you must be a new and different person, holy and good. Cloth yourself with this new nature."* Apostle Paul gives us the ways we can put on this new nature or self in Romans 12:1-2 and in Ephesians 4:22-32.

Again in the Book of Colossians, the apostle wrote: *"Since, then, you have been raised with Christ, set your hearts on things above, where Christ is seated at the right hand of God. Set your minds on things above, not on earthly things. For you died, and your life is now hidden with Christ in God. When Christ, who is your life, appears, then you also will appear with him in glory. Put to death, therefore, whatever belongs to your earthly nature: sexual immorality, impurity, lust, evil desires and greed, which is idolatry. Because of these, the wrath of God is coming. You used to walk in these ways, in the life you once lived. But now you must rid yourselves of all such things as these: anger, rage, malice, slander and filthy language from your lips. Do not lie to each other,* **since you have taken off your old self with its practices and have put on the new self,** *which is being renewed in knowledge in the image of its Creator"* (Col. 3:1-10).

Often it is not that easy to know if indeed we have put on the new self. Here also, Paul gave us guidance on how to ensure we have put on the new self; *"Therefore, as God's chosen people, holy and dearly loved, clothe yourselves with compassion, kindness, humility, gentleness and patience. Bear with each other and forgive whatever grievances you may have against one another. Forgive as the Lord forgave you. And over all these virtues put on love, which binds them all together in perfect unity. Let the peace of Christ rule in your hearts, since as members of one body you were called to peace. And be thankful. Let the word of Christ dwell in you richly as you teach and admonish one another with all wisdom, and as you sing psalms, hymns and spiritual songs with gratitude in your hearts to God. And whatever you do, whether in word or deed, do it all in the name of the Lord Jesus, giving thanks to God the Father through Him"* (Col. 3:12-17).

Let the peace of God reign in you.

The peace of God you enjoy, determines your height in the things of God. The peace of God is a gift of God, which we should jealously guard against the devil. It is the silent umpire within us that helps us, with our conscience, to determine what is right from wrong. Without peace, you may not be able to recall your dreams, and to a lesser extent visions also. This is a common reason why most people do not remember their dreams when they are troubled.

Have a good grip on your thought life.

Your thought life will eventually determine who you become. A thought is a seed for the future, and what you spend time on you make room for. Your thought life will be reflected in your dreams and visions.

Pay attention to things done at the close of each day.

At the close of each day, spend time meditating on the things of God. This will prepare your spiritual soil for whatever nightly encounters God may have for you.

Introduction to Dreams and Visions

Dreams come from God in the form of a parable language or illustrated stories. These personalized encoded messages are full of symbols that express the mysteries of God. As a result of the symbolism, dreams need some form of interpretation before a proper understanding can be gained. Interpretation can come to the dreamer either spontaneously, after praying to God about the dream, or through a person gifted in dream interpretation. Many people still hesitate to seek the meaning of their dreams, although it is biblical to do so; yet dream interpretation should be a carefully guided effort. Wrong interpretation has the potential to lead a person into bondage.

God utilizes very individualistic language in communicating to us in dreams. He takes it from our life experiences, specific personal traits, and biblical examples. God also uses events in our lives that no one knows about except Him, and sometimes incorporates these into His communications. So, a person gifted in dream interpretation can help with one's understanding, but correct interpretation must come from the dreamer due to a dream's specific, individualistic traits.

Contrary to the view that some people do not receive dreams, I believe that God speaks to everyone through them in one way or another. However, most people are unable to recall their dreams and, therefore, cannot appreciate their importance. Many people wonder why they do not receive many dreams. Some even claim that they do not dream at all, while others are simply at a loss at what to do with their endless amounts of dreams. These puzzles have no simple answers.

For more information on the fundamentals of Dreams and Visions see *Dreams and Visions Volume 1* by Dr. Joe Ibojie

POINTS TO PONDER

1. The more the church distances itself from understanding dreams and visions—valuable means of divine communication—the more it drives honest Christians into spiritual bondage. The world continually bombards believers and non-believers with occult literature and misinformation about dreams and visions. Are you willing to share the truth with the world?

2. Your greatest asset on earth is not only your ability to hear from God but also your ability to both hear and understand what God is saying to you. Dreams and visions are sure ways for God to direct the steps of the righteous believer and will remain ways to bring the agenda of Heaven to the earth. Are you listening for His voice and willing to take steps to understand?

3. For most people, divine inspiration may occur as a mere impression, or perhaps a prompting such as a flash of ideas, a picture, a birthing in the spirit, or even a knowing of conviction. However, you require maturity to distinguish what is of God and what is not. How mature are you in these matters?

Chapter 2

WHEN GOD SPEAKS
INTO YOUR SPIRIT

WHY ARE THERE HIDDEN MEANINGS
OF DREAMS AND VISIONS?

YOUR SPIRIT MAY KNOW something that could remain unknown to your mind, waiting for the divinely appointed time for it to unfold to your mind or consciousness. There are many instances of this in the Bible:

> But they did not understand what this meant. **It was hidden from them** so that they did not grasp it and they were afraid to ask Him about it (Luke 9:45).

Another example of this phenomenon is the story of the disciples on the way to Emmaus.

The Bible says that God kept the disciples from recognizing Jesus Christ but at the right time, their eyes were opened and the recognized Him:

> Now that same day two of them were going to a village called Emmaus, about seven miles from Jerusalem. They were talking with each other about everything that had happened. As they talked and discussed these things with each other, Jesus Himself came up and walked along

*with them; but **they were kept from recognizing Him*** (Luke 24:13-16).

*When He was at the table with them, He took bread, gave thanks, broke it and began to give it to them. **Then their eyes were opened** and they recognized Him, and He disappeared from their sight* (Luke 24:30-31).

After their eyes were opened to recognize Jesus Christ, *"they said to one another, **were not our hearts burning within us while He was speaking to us on the road,** while He was explaining the Scriptures to us"* (Luke 24:32). The moment they described as when their hearts were burning would have been the moment of the revelation to their spirits. But it was at that time unfruitful to their mind until they were at the table, when the Lord broke the bread and their minds were opened to the understanding.

Maybe that is why we have dreams with some scenes or areas of which we do not know the meaning. When this happens, I call this *hidden meaning* in dreams. Every dreamer will have dreams with hidden meanings or at least dreams with scenes or actions or symbols whose meaning are not clear. *Hidden meaning* in dreams and visions refers to the hidden things that are beyond human understanding and may be purposely sealed by the Holy Spirit until the set time. Most dreamers will have many of these, and until the Lord reveals their meaning, they remain obscured to the person.

Among the reasons why this may occur, is that hidden meanings may help keep the dreamer humble and reliant on the Holy Spirit at all times. Just like apostle Paul, the Bible says he received all surpassing revelations from God but in order to keep him humble, God allowed satan to afflict him with a thorn in his flesh, *"To keep me from becoming conceited because of these surpassingly great revelations, there was given me a thorn in my flesh, a messenger of Satan, to torment me"* (2 Cor. 12:7).

In some cases, hidden meanings in our dreams and visions are parts of what are regarded as the mysteries of God. A mystery is a truth that can only be divinely unfolded and is unknowable through reasoning. You have to be aware of something before you can realize that it is inexplicable. That awareness is the impartation in the spirit, but the understanding has to come to the mind. In practical terms, anything that arouses curiosity because it is unexplained, inexplicable, or secret is regarded as mysterious. It is the sovereignty of God to decide to whom He will unfold anything mysterious. It is also the prerogative of God to decide when and how much to reveal, where to reveal it, and also why reveal it at all. As the Bible says:

> *The secret things belong to the Lord our God, but the things revealed belong to us and to our children forever, that we may follow all the words of this law* (Deuteronomy 29:29).

> *The Lord our God has secrets known to no one. We are not accountable for them but we and our children are accountable for ever for all that He has revealed to us so that we obey all the terms of the instructions* (Deuteronomy 29:29 NLT).

In the Book of Revelation 1:1, the Bible reiterated the fact that there is always a reason why God reveals things to us: *"the Revelation of Jesus Christ, which God **gave Him to show to His servants.**"* The things that God revealed to apostle John were so that John might in turn show them to the servants of God.

When God reveals something, it immediately becomes fruitful to the spirit of the recipient. Our spirit bears witness with the Spirit of God. However, fruitfulness in the mind and therefore human understanding will wait for the appointed time for the understanding of what is revealed to the spirit man to come to the mind. Proper understanding at the mind-zone is necessary for the eventual fulfillment. Often the time of reception of the revelation in the spirit may differ from the time appointed for the understanding to come to our mind. This phenomenon is part of what is called *sealed mysteries* in the Bible and also explains why we may have hidden meanings in dreams, visions, and other revelations.

Therefore we should not be unduly worried if we cannot understand all that has been revealed, but move in faith and trust that at the right time God will give the fuller understanding. Apostle Paul lays credence to this principle when he spoke on a different subject, the subject of praying in tongues: *"For if I pray in an unknown tongue, my spirit prayeth, but my understanding is unfruitful"* (1 Cor. 14:14). So it is possible for the spirit to know something and yet be unknown in the mind. I believe many of us are able to survive the things that many others could not because God in

His infinite wisdom has endowed our spirits with divine substance through revelatory promises even though they may be unknown to our natural consciousness.

Why would God impart the human spirit and yet keep the person's mind from gaining meaningful understanding of the revelation? The reasons this may happen are many and I believe include the following:

- To impart the spirit of the person with destiny and yet save him or her from the "pride of life."

- To strengthen the spirit, so as to be able to rise to the challenges in times of trials.

- To save the person from compromising on Christian standards that can destroy the person's destiny. The inner witness keeps the person above difficult circumstances.

- To keep the spirit fervent, and yet keep emotion out of it, in calmness so that the person can wait for other events or people to be ready for their roles in the fulfillment of the destiny; otherwise human beings have the tendency to run ahead of the appointed time.

A fascinating example of when God speaks only to the spirit of a person is the story of the prophet Elijah and the widow of Zarephath. God clearly told the prophet to go Zarephath that He has *commanded* a widow to provide for him. When Elijah got there he met the widow all right, but her utterance did not show that she has received such instruction from God. At least it was unknown to her mind:

> *Then the word of the Lord came to him: "Go at once to Zarephath of Sidon and stay there.* **I have commanded a widow** *in that place to supply you with food"* (1 Kings 17:8-9).

> *So he went to Zarephath. When he came to the town gate, a widow was there gathering sticks. He called to her and asked, "Would you bring me a little water in a jar so I may have a drink?" As she was going to get it, he called, "And bring me, please, a piece of bread." "As surely as the Lord your God lives," she replied, "I don't have any bread—only a handful of flour in a jar and a little oil in a jug. I am gathering a few sticks to take home and make a meal for myself and*

my son, that we may eat it—and die." Elijah said to her, "Don't be afraid. Go home and do as you have said. But first make a small cake of bread for me from what you have and bring it to me, and then make something for yourself and your son. For this is what the Lord, the God of Israel, says: 'The jar of flour will not be used up and the jug of oil will not run dry until the day the Lord gives rain on the land.'" She went away and did as Elijah had told her. So there was food every day for Elijah and for the woman and her family. For the jar of flour was not used up and the jug of oil did not run dry, in keeping with the word of the Lord spoken by Elijah (1 Kings 17:10-16).

However, judging from the way she later responded and obeyed what seems a very difficult request, I conclude that request resonated in her spirit. In other words her spirit had been primed by God to obey and provide for Elijah even under that near impossible situation. It is possible that somehow God prepares us ahead of time to face certain challenging situations in life by intimating our spirit with the revelation ahead of the mind realization. Perhaps this helps to keep us from undue worries.

"This is that" phenomenon is very common; our ability to recognize them and take appropriate actions depends on our ability to hear the still small voice of God. In the case of prophet Samuel, being a seasoned Seer, the experience of his first meeting with Saul was a clear demonstration of this process probably because he was adept in the art of hearing God. God spoke to Samuel the night before he met Saul. When Samuel eventually met Saul, God prompted him saying, ***"This is the man I spoke to you about"***:

Now the day before Saul came, the Lord had revealed this to Samuel: "About this time tomorrow I will send you a man from the land of Benjamin. Anoint him leader over my people Israel; he will deliver My people from the hand of the Philistines. I have looked upon My people, for their cry has reached Me." When Samuel caught sight of Saul, the Lord said to him, "This is the man I spoke to you about; he will govern My people." Saul approached Samuel in the gateway and asked, "Would you please tell me where the seer's house is?" "I am the seer," Samuel replied. "Go up ahead of me to the high place, for today you are to eat with me, and in the morning I will let you go and will tell you all that is in your heart. As for the donkeys you lost three days ago, do not worry about them; they have been found. And to whom is all the desire of Israel turned, if not to you and all your father's family?" (1 Samuel 9:15-20).

Other scriptural examples include *apostle John's* experience: *"When the seven peals of thunder had spoken, I was about to write; and I heard a voice from heaven saying, 'Seal up the things which the seven peals of thunder have spoken and do not write them'"* (Rev. 10:4 NASB).

John was told to stop and seal up the message they spoke. We are not told why. The Bible gives no specific answer except that God didn't want these words to be fully revealed at that time. Though we should seek God for revelation and insight, God decides who and when to reveal things. However, later, apostle John was told not to seal the words of prophecy: *"Do not seal up the words of the prophecy of this book, because the time is near"* (Rev. 22:10).

Apostle Paul had a third heaven experience; he was not sure whether he was in body or out of the body when he heard things he was not permitted to speak.

> *I know a man in Christ who fourteen years ago—whether in the body I do not know, or out of the body I do not know, God knows— such a man was caught up to the third heaven...heard inexpressible words, which a man is not permitted to speak* (2 Corinthians 12:2-4 NASB).

Jesus Christ is the hidden wisdom of the age but destined to be revealed to us:

> *We do, however, speak a message of wisdom among the mature, but not the wisdom of this age or of the rulers of this age, who are coming to nothing. No, we speak of God's secret wisdom, a wisdom that has been hidden and that God destined for our glory before time began. None of the rulers of this age understood it, for if they had, they would not have crucified the Lord of glory"* (1 Corinthians 2:6-8).

Prophet Daniel had many of these sealed-up experiences as well:

> *The vision of the evenings and mornings that has been given you is true, but **seal up** the vision, for it concerns the distant future* (Daniel 8:26).

> *Go your way Daniel, because the words are **closed and sealed** until the time of the end. Many will be purified, made spotless and refined, but the wicked will continue to be wicked. None of the wicked will understand but those who are wise will understand* (Daniel 12:9-10).

> *But you, Daniel, **close up and seal the words** until the time of the end. Many will go here and thereto increase knowledge* (Daniel 12:4).

Zechariah and Daniel were both mightily used of God in revelatory realm. In fact, the Bible says of Daniel that he had understanding of all kinds of dreams and visions. Yet for both of these great prophets, we see many instances when they relied on an angelic interpreter to help them with the unfolding of the scenes with hidden meaning. In other words, to understand all dreams/visions means to possess the humility to seek relentlessly after what might not be clear in the dream. Sometimes, all you may need is the overall or panoramic view of the dream's meaning and keep on relying on the Holy Spirit to bring more light on your understanding as time progresses. For instance, certain symbol or symbolic actions or dream phrases will only unfold its details at the time of fulfillment. This has been my experience.

What to do while waiting for God to unfold the mystery or hidden meaning in dreams:

- Stay humble.
- Be obedient and accountable for what is unfolded to your understanding.
- Remain sensitive.
- Remain in the spirit.
- Seek Him for wisdom.
- Seek for His love and for who He is.

- Study the Word.

- Do not forsake the assembly of the saints.

- Don't be discouraged.

- Be confident that at the appropriate time God will unfold the mystery.

WHEN GOD IS SILENT

I define the *silence of God* as when communication with God on an individual level is withheld or restricted. God may be silent on a personal level even though an open heaven exists in place. One example of when God is said to be silent is when there is excessive prolongation of the normal season of low dream or vision reception. The silence of God could also mean that God is deliberately not communicating with the person, or God is speaking but the person is hindered because he is stereotyped in his expectation of how to hear from God.

Sometimes the perceived silence may be due to lack of understanding about what God is saying, like in the case of Job. God spoke to Job in dreams: *"For God does speak—now one way, now another—though man may not perceive it. In a dream, in a vision of the night, when deep sleep falls on men as they slumber in their beds"* (Job 33:14-15). We know Job did not perceive it because he also said: *"If only I knew where to find him [God]; if only I could go to His dwelling! I would state my case before Him and fill my mouth with arguments. I would find out what He would answer me, and consider what He would say"* (Job 23:3-5).

God is never really silent. As the prophet Isaiah said, *"Surely the arm of the Lord is not too short to save, nor His ears too dull to hear"* (Isa. 59:1). We may be unable to hear Him at times for one reason or the other. There is normal seasonal variation in the dreamer's ability to receive dreams and visions. The seasonal variation in dream reception is explained in my first book, *Dreams and Visions: How to Receive, Interpret and Apply Your Dreams.*

Consider the following during silence of God times:

- God withdraws into what appears to be silent mode in order to teach you to hear His many other ways of communicating, other than the one you are used to.

- More importantly, God can withdraw from you because of sin in your life: *"your iniquities have separated you from your God; and your sins have hidden His face from you, so that He will not hear"* (Isa. 59:2).

- However, it is wrong to assume that whenever you feel that God is silent that it is because of sin. Nevertheless, it always advisable to begin searching for the solution with repentance.

- The silence of God should not be a time to be discouraged or the time to quit, but a time to trust Him.

- Silence does not mean absence. He is always with you. This is the time to recall to the mind what the Bible says: *"What I tell you in the dark, speak in the daylight; what is whispered in your ear, proclaim from the roofs"* (Matt. 10:27).

- The time of His silence in your life could be transformed into a time of equipping if correctly utilized.

- The prophet Isaiah gives another reason God may be silent when he says, *"Truly You are a God who hides Himself. O God and Savior of Israel"* (Isa. 45:15). Maybe God just loves to hide and watch as we search for Him?

Surviving the Silence of God

To survive the silence of God it is important to keep the following in mind:

- Keep your focus on God.
- Keep to His last perceived commandment.
- Maintain a childlike spiritual simplicity.
- Be at the post of your responsibility.
- Avoid presumptuous acts.

In the Book of Deuteronomy, the Bible speaks of the Heaven over a person's head that could become closed as a consequence of sin in the person's life: *"The **heavens over your head will be** [brass] **bronze**, the ground beneath you iron"* (Deut. 28:23).

The following seven ways can facilitate the opening of Heaven over a person's head or break the silence of God:

1. Obedience to the will of God.

At the baptism of Jesus Christ, the Heaven opened when Jesus, in obedience to the will of God, humbled Himself to be baptized by John the Baptist: *"Then Jesus came from Galilee to the Jordan to be baptized by John. But John tried to deter Him, saying, "I need to be baptized by You, and do You come to me?" Jesus replied, "Let it be so now; it is proper for us to do this to fulfill all righteousness." Then John consented. As soon as Jesus was baptized, He went up out of the water. At that moment heaven was opened, and He saw the Spirit of God descending like a dove and lighting on Him. And a voice from heaven said, "This is my Son, whom I love; with Him I am well pleased"* (Matt. 3:13-17).

2. Faith in God.

Jesus told Nathaniel that he would see Heaven open as he continues to believe: *"Jesus said, 'You believe because I told you I saw you under the fig tree. You shall see greater things than that." He then added, "I tell you the truth, you shall see heaven open, and the angels of God ascending and descending on the Son of Man"* (John 1:50-51).

3. Faithful in offering and tithes.

When the floodgates (windows) of Heaven are opened, God pours out not only material blessings but also revelations: *"Bring the whole tithe into the storehouse, that there may be food in My house. Test Me in this," says the Lord Almighty, "and see if I will not throw open the floodgates of heaven and pour out so much blessing that you will not have room enough for it"* (Mal. 3:10).

4. Prayers and gifts to the poor.

Heaven opened upon Cornelius, a known Gentile, and he recieved angelic visitation because of his generosity to those in need and his prayerfulness: *"He and all his family were devout and God-fearing; he gave generously to those in need and prayed to God regularly. One day at about three in the afternoon he had a vision. He distinctly saw an angel of God, who came to him and said, 'Cornelius!' Cornelius stared at him in fear. 'What is it, Lord?' he asked. The angel answered, 'Your prayers and gifts to the poor have come up as a memorial offering before God'"* (Acts 10:2-4).

5. Sacrifice.

King Solomon offered so much sacrifice that God called his temple a temple of sacrifice in an open heaven experience: *"The king went to Gibeon to offer sacrifices, for that was the most important high place, and Solomon offered a thousand burnt offerings on that altar. At Gibeon the Lord appeared to Solomon during the night in a dream, and God said, 'Ask for whatever you want me to give you'"* (1 Kings 3:4-5). Also, *"The Lord appeared to him at night and said: 'I have heard your prayer and have chosen this place for myself as a temple for sacrifices'"* (2 Chron. 7:12).

6. Prayer and fasting.

Second Chronicles 7 says, *"if My people, who are called by My name, will humble themselves and pray and seek My face and turn from their wicked ways, then will I hear from heaven and will forgive their sin and will heal their land"* (2 Chron. 7:14).

Apostle Peter's mindset that salvation belongs only to the Jews was broken in an open heaven encounter with God, following a fast and prayer period: *"About noon the following day as they were on their journey and approaching the city, Peter went up on the roof to pray. He became hungry and wanted something to eat, and while the meal was being prepared, he fell into a trance. He saw heaven opened and something like a large sheet being let down to earth by its four corners. It contained all kinds of four-footed animals, as well as reptiles of the earth and birds of the air"* (Acts 10:9-12).

7. Applying the blood of the Lamb.

Underpinning all the privileges to receive open heaven experiences is the fact that the blood of Christ has made the way to the Holy of Holies: *"He did not enter by means of the blood of goats and calves; but he entered the Most Holy Place once for all by His own blood, having obtained eternal redemption"* (Heb. 9:12).

POINTS TO PONDER

1. Your spirit may know something that could remain unknown to your mind, waiting for the divinely appointed time for it to unfold to your mind or consciousness. Have you experienced this type of circumstance?

   _____

   _____

2. Hidden meanings in your dreams and visions are parts of what are regarded as the mysteries of God. It is the sovereignty of God to decide to whom He will unfold anything mysterious. It is also the prerogative of God to decide when and how much to reveal, where to reveal it, and also why reveal it at all. Are you willing to wait on God's timing?

   _____

   _____

3. To survive the silence of God it is important to keep the following in mind: Keep your focus on God. Keep to His last perceived commandment. Maintain a childlike spiritual simplicity. Be at the post of your responsibility. Avoid presumptuous acts. How easy—or hard—is it for you to follow this advice?

   _____

   _____

Chapter 3

KEY FACTS
ABOUT DREAMS

IN MY EXPERIENCE I have found the following facts and Scriptures to be key when exploring dreams and their meanings.

- The Bible is central to understanding the meaning of dream symbols.

- Spiritual truths are spiritually discerned: *"This is what we speak, not in words taught us by human wisdom but in words taught by the Spirit, expressing spiritual truths in spiritual words"* (1 Cor. 2:13).

- Spiritual truths cannot be taught by human wisdom: *"And we are setting these truths forth in words not taught by human wisdom but taught by the [Holy] Spirit, combining and interpreting spiritual truths with spiritual language [to those who possess the Holy Spirit]"* (1 Cor. 2:13 AMP).

- Non-Christians cannot understand "Holy Spirit facts" because they are taught by the Holy Spirit: *"So we use the Holy Spirit's words to explain the Holy Spirit's facts. But the man who is not a Christian can't understand and can't accept these thoughts from God, which the Holy Spirit teaches us. They sound foolish to him, because only those who have the Holy Spirit within them can understand what the Holy Spirit means. Others just can't take it in. But the spiritual man has insight into everything, and that bothers and baffles the man of the world, who can't understand him at all. How could he? Certainly, he has never been one to know the Lord's thoughts, or to discuss them with Him or to move the hands of God by prayers. But, strange as it seems, we Christians actually do have within us a portion of the very thoughts and mind of God* (1 Cor. 2:13b-16 TLB).

LESSONS FROM DANIEL 1:17

- Knowledge and understanding as a gift from God.
- Ability to acquire knowledge as a gift from God.
- Wisdom is a product of the study of the Word of God.
- Understanding of dreams and visions as a result of the combination of the above.

To these four young men God gave knowledge and understanding of all kinds of literature and learning. And Daniel could understand visions and dreams of all kinds (Daniel 1:17).

And *"There is a man in your kingdom that has the spirit of the holy gods in him. In the time of your father he was found to have insight and intelligence and wisdom like that of the gods. King Nebuchadnezzar your father—your father the king, I say— appointed him chief of the magicians, enchanters, astrologers and diviners. This man Daniel, whom the king called Belteshazzar, was found to have a keen mind and knowledge and understanding, and also the ability to interpret dreams, explain riddles and solve difficult problems. Call for Daniel, and he will tell you what the writing means"* (Dan. 5:11-12).

- The Book of Revelation can only be understood within the context of the imagery of the Old Testament.

INTERPRETATION OF DREAMS

Interpretation should not be reduced to a series of dos and don'ts. There is no formula for getting the meaning of dream; it is a supernatural quickening, an off-shoot of divine wisdom given to man by the Holy Spirit. I have found the following key facts pivotal to proper understanding of dreams:

- *Absolute dependency on God.* In Genesis 40:8 we're told, *"We both had dreams,"* they answered, *"but there is no one to interpret them." Then Joseph said to them, "Do not interpretations belong to God? Tell me your dreams."* Here Joseph is absolutely confident that God will help him gain understanding of their dreams. And he showed the same reliance on God's guidance when he spoke to Pharaoh, *"it is not me, God will give Pharaoh an answer of peace"* (Gen. 41:16). This is similar to what Jesus Christ promised His disciples, *"But make up your mind not to worry beforehand how you will defend yourselves. For I will give you words and wisdom that none of your adversaries will be able to resist or contradict"* (Luke 21:14-15). They were to depend on Him to provide the right word for them to speak at the right time.

- *Faith that God will give the wisdom for interpretation.* Daniel had faith and declared to Nebuchadnezzar that, *"The king asked Daniel (also called Belteshazzar), 'Are you able to tell me what I saw in my dream and interpret it?' Daniel replied, 'No wise man, enchanter, magician or diviner can explain to the king the mystery he has asked about, but there is a God in heaven who reveals mysteries. He has shown King Nebuchadnezzar what will happen in days to come...'"* (Dan. 2:26-28). Also the Bible says, *"If any of you lacks wisdom, he should ask God, who gives generously to all without finding fault, and it will be given to him. But when he asks, he must believe and not doubt, because he who doubts is like a wave of the sea, blown and tossed by the wind. That man should not think he will receive anything from the Lord"* (James 1:5-7).

- Also, the dynamics of how dreams are released to the mind from the dreamer's spirit is enhanced by the dreamer's faith in God. Without faith, revelations will remain dormant in the spirit. Once a revelation is processed in the mind, proper comprehension and correlation to the dreamer's circumstance is influenced by the peace and godly liberty the dreamer enjoys.

- *Ask for wisdom to gain the main essence of the dream.* Joseph and Daniel were great interpreters of dreams and demonstrated good grasp of the essence of the dreams they interpreted. As a result they were able to give wise counsel to the dreamers. *"Therefore, O king, be pleased to accept my advice: Renounce your sins by doing what is right, and your wickedness by being kind to the oppressed. It may be that then your prosperity will continue"* (Dan. 4:27). *"And now let Pharaoh look for a discerning and wise man and put him in charge of the land of Egypt. Let Pharaoh appoint commissioners over the land to take a fifth of the harvest of Egypt during the seven years of abundance. They should collect all the food of these good years that are coming and store up the grain under the authority of Pharaoh, to be kept in the cities for food. This food should be held in reserve for the country, to be used during the seven years of famine that will come upon Egypt, so that the country may not be ruined by the famine.' The plan seemed good to Pharaoh and to all his officials"* (Gen. 41:33-37).

- *Interpretation must be Bible-guided.* The spiritual truth expressed in dreams needs to be understood by spiritual words contained in the Bible. *"We have not received the spirit of the world but the **Spirit who is from God, that we may understand what God has freely given us.** This is what we speak, not in words taught us by human wisdom **but in words taught by the Spirit, expressing spiritual truths in spiritual words.** The man without the Spirit does not accept the things that come from the Spirit of God, for they are foolishness to him, and he cannot understand them, because they are spiritually discerned"* (1 Cor. 2:12-14).

- *Study the Word of God to obtain divine knowledge and wisdom.* Daniel's giftedness in dream interpretation was enhanced by his skills in acquiring knowledge and his being well-versed in all kinds of literature. The more we study the Bible, the better we become in dream interpretation. *"To these four young men God gave knowledge and understanding of all kinds of literature and learning. And Daniel could understand visions and dreams of all kinds"* (Dan. 1:17).

- *Always look for Bible phrases, actions, or imagery that might have occurred in the dream.* These Bible phrases or actions are often the promptings of the Holy Spirit regarding the essence of the revelation. The first and most important response to a revelation, is to pray for all the elements, events, and persons (friends and perceived enemies) that play a part in the revelation—do this even before you gain an understanding of the meaning of the revelation.

- *Other key points.* A revelation may occur and be remembered in fragments. In most of these cases, God wants to focus on, or emphasize, the remembered fragment. It may also be an indication of poor reception due to sin or prayerlessness on the part of the dreamer. A dreamer who is a watchman is endowed by God to see things from afar and warn the people about things before they actually happen.

Interpretation given in the revelation needs to be properly studied, as both the revelation and the interpretation may need further interpretation. The clearer the dream revelation, the greater is the responsibility to act on it and the greater is the enemy's opposition.

DREAM CLUES

The following "clues" may help dreamers when trying to understand the meaning of their dreams.

- Any lingering emotion from the dream; *something from the dream encounter that sticks with the dreamer.*

- Anything out of the usual or the expected; *this may indicate that something unexpected is coming the dreamer's way*

- Inappropriate responses; *these may be to draw the dreamer's attention to what may otherwise have gone unnoticed or things that may not be what they appear to be on the surface. The inappropriateness may in fact be the true thing that has been covered up. Also may hint at the symbolic nature of the dream.*

- Incongruous feeling on the part of the dreamer or incongruous reaction from other people; *may mean to be careful, things may not be what they seem or it may be to alert the dreamer to the symbolic nature of the dream.*

- Dream phrases heard; *these are to be carefully studied in line with the Word of God.*

- The setting or background of most scenes in the dream; *this helps to determine the aspects of the dreamer's life addressed in the dream.*

- Scenes of confusion or forgetfulness; *these may often indicate inner uncertainty or indecision in the life of the dreamer.*

- Emotion, pains, joy, fear, etc. in the dream; *in most cases they are often literal but what is usually more important is the degree or the intensity of the expression. For instance, crying in a dream may just help to indicate the deep emotional involvement when the events eventually occur in real life.*

- The people in the dream; *the majority of people in dreams are symbolic.*

- Scenes that portray surprises of either pleasantness or unpleasantness *are often clues.*

- Urgency with which events might have occurred; *this may be event-play just we have word-play that indicate the need for speed in real life to avoid missing divinely set timing.*

- Take note of the concluding emotion that prevailed in the dream or concluding statement that the dreamer woke up with; *the dreamer's response ultimately at the fulfillment of the dream.*

PEACE OF MIND AFTER DREAM ENCOUNTER

Maintaining peace and retreating into one's spirit should be a planned and deliberate action on the part of the dreamer if he is to avoid emotional backlash following a dream or visionary encounter. This is often the singular most important factor that challenges the dreamer on the path to gaining proper understanding of his dreams. Quite often, emotions run high when the dreamer awakes from a dream about himself or about the family. I have often taken the following steps, to overcome this hurdle.

Listen in the spirit:

- Calm my mind in the Lord's presence.
- Use the eyes of my faith; walk by faith and not by sight.
- Trust that God will give me the correct understanding.
- Allow the peace of God to rule my mind and heart.
- Wait for prompting of the Holy Spirit.

Put away acts of the soul realm:

- Don't allow intellect and logic to rule my mind.

- Don't entertain fear and confusion.
- Don't become apprehensive or anxious.
- Don't allow emotions from the dream to cloud my judgment.
- Try to keep a clear mind.

A Spiritually Weak Dreamer

From the fallen state to the redemption of man, the human spirit exists at two levels: an *unregenerate spirit* (the spirit of man in the fallen state of man) and *regenerated spirit*, the spirit of man after redemption by the blood of Jesus Christ (the born-again Christian's state). However, the regenerated spirit of man can either be weak or strong, and the strength of the human spirit determines whether or not the person is able to war successfully in the spirit.

A weak human spirit is a regenerated spirit of man that is not sustained in the consistent power of the Word of God and is not dwelling in the presence of God with a conscience not maintained in the constant washing in the blood of Jesus. The hallmarks of this weakness in the spirit of the dreamer include:

- Blurred visions or dreams.
- Unusually docile and poor participating roles in dreams or visions, or lack of righteous firmness during dream encounters.
- Fragmented dreams; dreams remembered only in bits and pieces.
- Prolonged period of inability to recall dreams.
- Poor rendering of dreams and visions so that it is not useful to those that dreams are meant to help.

Communion with God strengthens the human spirit, the wisdom of God also empowers the human spirit and the spirit of man is also built up by sanctification of the human conscience. The following important steps strengthen the human spirit:

- Studying the Bible; life application of the Word of God is wisdom.
- Praying and fasting; breaks the outer man to allow the spirit man to be fully expressed.
- Paying attention to your tithes and offerings; opens the window of Heaven for you.

- Spending quality time with God; reduces the hardening effect of natural living on emotion, human will power, and mindsets. When you spend time with God, you become less emotional.

CHANGING DREAMS FROM MONOLOGUE TO DIALOGUE

This is the process in which the dreamer can dialogue with God by dream communications.

Dialoguing with God in dreams often takes the form of a series of dreams in which the dreamer awakens between dreams and intercedes in response to the preceding dream. God then replies to the dreamer's response with another dream and so continues the discussion. Actually this phenomenon is common, but most people miss out on it because they regard them as repeat dreams. I believe that Joseph's (of the coat of many colors) dreams were a pair of dialoguing dreams in which God used the second dream to correct the restricted perspectives of Joseph's view of the promised rulership (see Gen. 37:1-11). Joseph was not just going to lord it over his brothers, but his rulership would cover the then known world, hence the moon and the sun in the second dream. In the Book of Genesis, the moon and the sun are rulers. The Bible says "the sun to rule the day and the moon to rule the night."

To be able to change from monologue to dialogue in dream communication, the dreamer needs to first of all develop the art of recording dream encounters and reviewing them regularly. This will provide the background to enable the dreamer to pick up issues that might have been missed in a single dream and its interpretation. Second, the following steps will help the dreamer dialogue in dream communications; the essence here is that God rewards the effort of appropriate responses from the dreamer with furtherance of the discussion He has initiated:

- Ask God for clarification on areas that are not clear in the dream encounter.
- Have faith that God will give the answer, that He will hear and respond.
- Be sensitive in the spirit to pick answers to questions asked; whether in further dreams or visions or any other form of revelation.
- Live a life of prayers and intercession.

- Seek the mercy and grace of God at all times; it is by His grace that we are who we are.
- Seek the wisdom of God at all times by studying the Word of God.
- A life of fasting and sacrifice sharpens one's dream life.

RECOGNIZING UNIQUE PATTERNS OF DREAM DRAMATIZATION

Over the years as I have interpreted dreams for other people, I could in most cases sense uniqueness in the drama patterns of some dreamers. I have often wondered about this, and I have come to discern some uniqueness in the pattern of individual dream dramatization.

In the Book of Daniel, God gave dreams of the future empires that would arise on Babylon to both King Nebuchadnezzar and the prophet Daniel but with unique individual dramatization. For the king, who conquered many nations and collected precious metals from them, God used gold, silver, and bronze as symbols mirroring perhaps the special preoccupation of the king (the dream of a large statue; see Dan. 2:32). But for Daniel, God used animals (the dream of the four beasts; see Dan. 7:4-7). Animals were common symbols in Daniel's dreams and visions. Nevertheless, the two dreams essentially spoke of the same message.

Let us look at the unique dramatization pattern of some dreamers in the Bible and the noticeable characteristics of their dreams.

Joseph, earthly father of Jesus
- Directional and personal
- Short, sharp, full of phrases
- Angelic interactions
- Minimal symbolism

Jacob
- Directional and personal

Daniel
- Directional and governmental
- Animals

Paul

- Directional and reveals God's plans/purposes
- Probably had a third heaven translation
- Short, sharp

Factors that may influence uniqueness in dream dramatization include:

- Uniqueness of the call on the person.
- Prevailing circumstances in the dreamer's life.
- Whether or not the dreamer has an erroneous mindset that needs correction.
- What God might want to say.

A personal testimony about dream dramatization or pattern: *There is a couple—very close family friends—and we have often shared our dreams for better understanding. Consequently, we learned a lot about each other's dreams. One day, the husband shared a dream with me. His wife was not present on that occasion. However, I recognized the pattern was more characteristic of his wife's dreams, so I asked, "Is that your wife's dream?" The answer was "Yes!"*

Dreams are written in fading ink. This is how Job described a dream: *"Like a dream he flies away, no more to be found, banished like a vision of the night"* (Job 20:8). This is also what the Psalmist says, *"We glide along the tides of times as swiftly as a racing river and vanish as quickly as a dream"* (Ps. 90:5 TLB).

The Danger of Shallow Understanding of Dreams

The problem of poor and partial understanding of revelations has become more rampant these days than ever before and continues to be a clear and present danger despite biblical examples of its dire consequences. Everywhere I go, this danger looms and some people have gone diagonally opposite the divine wisdom inherent in their revelation because of shallow understanding.

A personal testimony about this danger: *I am the senior pastor of our church. I once had a dream that a trusted member of the congregation was making uncomplimentary remarks about me. I pondered on this for some weeks. While thinking about this, I maintained my usual relationship with this person. Soon the person started to behave as I have seen in the dream, despite all my prayers. I sought the face of God on this issue. Then the Holy Spirit ministered to me that the purpose of the dream was to alert me to possible misinformation received by the person that I should correct before it gave rise to bitterness. I have now done that and the church, the person, and myself are all the better for it.*

God will not show us a dream to start a war in a congregation or in a family. Whenever God gives us dreams that warn us of other people's anger or animosity toward us, at least sometimes, it is so that we can address the possible cause of the situation or behavior. We should seek to correct any imbalance rather than rush into defensive mode, which may ultimately mean retaliatory moves. If we handle it in a godly way, through the process we could gain back the brother or the friend.

It was because of shallow and partial understanding that Joseph's brothers (of the coat of many colors) sold him into slavery. They fought bitterly against the very gift that was meant to save them from perishing in famine. If they had pondered on the revelations given to them by God through the dreams that Joseph had received, they would have found that their obeisance toward him was part of Joseph's rulership of the entire world and that this was the means by which God would preserve them and the entire people of Israel.

NATURAL OCCURRENCES CAN CONFIRM DREAM REVELATIONS

Things can happen in a real-life situation that appears to re-enact the events of a dream or a vision. Many people have had dreams and visions that were followed by identical real-life happenings, as if the dream or the vision were acted out in front of them. The questions are: was the dream or vision fulfilled in that natural happening or was the natural happening only a confirmation of the revelation? In the latter case, the revelation will have its true fulfillment at a future time. Commonly, the natural happening is not the fulfillment but a re-affirmation of what is being communicating to the person.

In my experience, some real-life happenings after a revelation sometimes serve as a confirmation of the revelation, which then is followed by the true fulfillment at a later date. This is much the same principle as in the repetition of Pharaoh's dream that Joseph explained: *"The reason the dream was given to Pharaoh in two forms is that the matter has been firmly decided by God, and God will do it soon"* (Gen. 41:32).

My own conclusion on this issue is that if the natural happening was able to answer the crucial question (why the dream or vision is given to the person) it most probably was part of the fulfillment. Otherwise it should be a confirmation of the revelation that would still have its fulfillment at a later date.

CLUSTERING IN DREAM REVELATIONS

There is phenomenon that I've observed over the years as I have studied prophetic symbolism. There are times when many people who are related or connected in some way, receive the same message around the same time, although it may be dramatized with individual variations. For instance, a river bursting its banks may play up in the dreams of many people within a certain geographical location. This is often a reflection of the divine message in the spiritual atmosphere surrounding the people.

Pharaoh versus the butler and the baker.

The scenario was that Pharaoh's birth date was three days away. He decided on a plan of action including the fate of two of his servants who were then in jail. He decided to restore the butler but to execute the baker on his birthday.

- This powerful king firmly finalized his decisions, though unknown to these servants, his decisions were therefore sealed in the spirit realm.
- God, however, relayed the message in dreams to them. Both servants had dreams relating to the fate that was to befall them.
- The messages were relayed to both servants from the spiritual atmosphere and the dreams or messages were clustered to both of them in one night.

Apostle Paul and disciple Ananias versus the anointing and healing of apostle Paul's blindness.

- Paul dreamt that Ananias laid hands on him (see Acts 9:11-12). Ananias had the vision to go lay hands on Paul (see Acts 9:10-18). The message was clustered to both of them each as the message concerns him even though they were in different locations.

Apostle Peter and Cornelius—the conversion of the first Gentile.

- Cornelius had a vision to send for Peter (see Acts 10:1-6).

- Peter's vision was to accept the Gentiles and accept the invitation to go to Cornelius's house (see Acts 10:9-19).

A Personal Testimony. *At a dream clinic in Glasgow, Scotland, three members of a family each had dream of snakes in one single night. Few weeks later, this family came under very horrendous accusations but Jesus Christ delivered them. Snakes may be symbolic of impending accusations in dreams.*

THE VALUE OF DREAMS

Dreams have value even if they are not remembered. A classical example was the dream of the large statue that Nebuchadnezzar had. He knew it was in his spirit but his mind could not recall it. In this case, it was due to issues in the king's life. Such issues most likely include sinfulness, busyness, prayerlessness, and lack of peace, to name a few. However, inability to remember dreams in a few cases could also be due an act of God, akin to the experience of certain disciples of Christ on the way to Emmaus, when God deliberately withheld them from recognizing Jesus Christ. As mentioned previously, the Bible says that God held them back from recognizing Jesus Christ until they were at the table with Him when their eyes supernaturally opened to recognize Him. Then they said, "Didn't our hearts burn within" when they journeyed with Him. In other wards, they knew in the realm of spirit that they were in the company of God because their hearts burned within them, though they could not fully understand it in their minds at that time.

There are possible benefits of dreams that are sealed in our spirit even when we cannot recall them to our memory. Benefits may include:

- Spiritual familiarity or "this is that" phenomenon occurs when eventually we face the situation in real life, when we may be prompted to realize that this is that we have seen in the spirit.

- To instill inner awareness of who we really are—the awareness of the promises and the plans of God revealed to our inner being.

- Familiarity in the spirit removes the drastic impact of suddenness that changes may bring when the event eventually happens in real life.
- Inner awareness provides a place of peace in moments of crisis.

DREAM WITHIN A DREAM

The inner dream or vision, a dream or vision within a dream, for me is often a higher level of or purer revelation. From my experience, it would appear that the dreamer is also opened up to God for greater in-depth (unfolding) of the mysteries of God. This is because the dreamer is then in a dream environment where the influences of the soul and mind are restricted. The dreamer's spirit is in a purer and sharper spiritual receptiveness and also better placed to discern. It is generally a more spiritual encounter. In the inner dream, because of the fewer influences from the soul realm and the body, the dream is in purer communication with divinity. Scriptural examples include Abraham's dream within vision in Genesis 15:12-19 and Ezekiel's vision within a vision found in Ezekiel 8:9-11,14-15.

In some ways, dreams within dreams are like prophecy within prophecy (the same principles apply):

> *Therefore my heart is glad and my tongue rejoices; my body also will rest secure, because You will not abandon me to the grave, nor will You let your Holy One see decay. You have made known to me the path of life; You will fill me with joy in Your presence, with eternal pleasures at Your right hand* (Psalm 16:9-11).

In this Psalm, David transcends during the prophecy in this passage into prophecy about Jesus' death and resurrection.

In prophesying about the king of Tyre, the prophet Ezekiel also shed light into the fate that befell satan by the word of knowledge.

> *The word of the Lord came to me: "Son of man, take up a lament concerning the king of Tyre and say to him: 'This is what the Sovereign Lord says: " 'You were the model of perfection, full of wisdom and perfect in beauty. You were in Eden, the garden of God; every precious*

stone adorned you: ruby, topaz and emerald, chrysolite, onyx and jasper, sapphire, turquoise and beryl. Your settings and mountings were made of gold; on the day you were created they were prepared. You were anointed as a guardian cherub, for so I ordained you. You were on the holy mount of God; you walked among the fiery stones. You were blameless in your ways from the day you were created till wickedness was found in you. Through your widespread trade you were filled with violence, and you sinned. So I drove you in disgrace from the mount of God, and I expelled you, O guardian cherub, from among the fiery stones. Your heart became proud on account of your beauty, and you corrupted your wisdom because of your splendour. So I threw you to the earth; I made a spectacle of you before kings. By your many sins and dishonest trade you have desecrated your sanctuaries. So I made a fire come out from you, and it consumed you, and I reduced you to ashes on the ground in the sight of all who were watching. All the nations who knew you are appalled at you; you have come to a horrible end and will be no more" (Ezekiel 28:11-19).

Characteristics of inner dreams and visions that I have observed:

- Sharper
- Purer revelation
- Deeper revelation
- More mysteries are unfolded
- Greater insightful knowledge may be revealed
- Less influences from the human soul

When interpreting dreams within dreams, interpret the inner dream before interpreting the outer dream and often you apply the outer dream before applying the inner dream.

Visionary Dreams and the Voice Phenomenon

Phrases are often heard in *revelatory encounters*. Each phrase should be recorded exactly as heard. They are often divine insights into a situation that run far beyond the limits of human verbal communication. However, revelatory phrases that run contrary to the Scriptures are not from God, no matter how smooth, appropriate, alluring and wise they may sound. In the Book of Luke, we see where the Scriptures were twisted by the devil: *"The devil led Him to Jerusalem and had Him stand on the highest point of the temple. "If You are the Son of God," he said, "throw Yourself down from here. For it is written: "'He will command His angels concerning You to guard You carefully; they will lift You up in their hands, so that You will not strike your foot against a stone."' Jesus answered, "It says: 'Do not put the Lord your God to the test"* (Luke 4:9-12). The quote was correct but the suggestions and insinuations were contrary to the principles inherent in Scriptures.

On the other hand, revelatory phrases from God are often clear, short and sharp; most require prompt attention and action. Revelatory phrases that require immediate and prompt action will often come with no ambiguity or complex symbolism.

However, voices in our revelations should be carefully discerned. The voice of God will bear witness with the spirit of the person like a knowing in the inner being that God is stirring something in the person by voicing the fact or truth. The Bible says, "My sheep hear My voice and the voice of another they will not follow" and *"But you have an anointing from the Holy One, and all of you know the truth"* (1 John 2:20). We have the anointing of the Holy Spirit, the seal of God within to tell us the truth.

Furthermore, phrases from the second heaven—the devil and his agents—will bear hallmarks of the devil. Somehow in the person's subconscious mind, something will not sit correctly regarding what was said, or there will be a deep reservation about the information.

It is important that you record these phrases exactly as you have heard them without trying to rationalize the phrase.

The following Scripture passages contain examples of God's voice breaking into dreams or visions: Acts 11:1-14, Ezekiel 37, and Daniel 4:4-17.

The different types of divine proclamations that commonly break into our dreams include:

- Decreed events; things that are ordained to happen, regardless of human action.
- Proclamation of paradigm shift; announcing to humankind the need to prepare or adjust for what God wants to do or is doing.

- To provide a lingering echo; a soft, gentle, and persistent reminder.

Various sources of the voice in dreams and visions:

- When God speaks into the dream or vision directly or as a voice from the expanse of the sky or as the voice of an angel.
- The voice of other people.
- The voice of the devil and his agents.

Therefore, every revelatory phrase needs to be subjected to the following tests:

- First, does it line up with the Scriptures?
- Second, does it pass the love test? It should speak of love because God is love.
- Finally, does what you hear pass the wisdom test? The ultimate test for wisdom from God is if it has respect for human lives no matter whose life is involved.

In general, when we record phrases from God we encourage God to give more.

MULTIPLE APPLICATIONS

Often many dreamers find immediate application of the meaning of their dreams but only to find another, and perhaps even more important, application on a later date. *Prophetic messages* often have double or multiple applications—one for the people who first heard the message and another deeper application for a future time. In the same way, most *dreams* may exhibit immediate application to the prevailing circumstance but have another and perhaps much deeper application in a future date. It is important to add at this juncture, that from my experience, a ***dream always has a one meaning but the divine principle in the dream's meaning may be applicable on more than one occasion***. God speaks and uses the prophets first by imparting them with the essence of the prophetic message and then through them to impart to other people. Therefore a basic and useful principle is to first apply any dream to the dreamer before applying it to others or giving it a wider perspective.

One can discern this spiritual principle in operation in the following passage: *"Jesus answered and said to them, destroy this temple and in three days I will raise it up. Then the Jews said, it has taken forty-six years to build this temple and will you raise it* *up in three days, **but He was speaking of the temple of His body***" (John 2:19-21). In this prophetic statement Jesus was speaking of His resurrection after three days in the grave but at the same time that principle was equally applicable to the destruction of the actual temple that was to come many years later.

The stories that Jesus Christ told during His earthly ministry had powerful multiple applications. His parable stories can relate to people in different ways. For instance, the different soils in the parable of the sower (see Matt. 13:1-25) may be heard differently by four people or the same individual at various stages of life depending on how one identifies with the soils described in the story.

Similarly the story of "the lost son" in Luke 15:11-35 will affect a father quite differently from a rebellious son or a jealous brother. More importantly, even at different times in the life of a single individual, the person can pass through the phase of feeling like a prodigal son, like the jealous elder brother, and the phase of being a father.

Another classic example is when a prophet gave prophecy to Eli, the priest at Shiloh, about the judgment of God upon his family:

> *Now Eli, who was very old, heard about everything his sons were doing to all Israel and how they slept with the women who served at the entrance to the Tent of Meeting. So he said to them, "Why do you do such things? I hear from all the people about these wicked deeds of yours. No, my sons; it is not a good report that I hear spreading among the Lord's people. If a man sins against another man, God may mediate for him; but if a man sins against the Lord, who will intercede for him?" His sons, however, did not listen to their father's rebuke, for it was the Lord's will to put them to death. And the boy Samuel continued to grow in stature and in favor with the Lord and with men. Now a man of God came to Eli and said to him, "This is what the Lord says: 'Did I not clearly reveal Myself to your father's house when they were in Egypt under Pharaoh? I chose your father out of all the tribes of Israel to be My priest, to go up to My altar, to burn incense, and to wear an ephod in my presence. I also gave your father's house all the offerings made with fire by the Israelites. Why do you scorn My sacrifice and offering that I prescribed for My dwelling?*

Why do you honor your sons more than Me by fattening yourselves on the choice parts of every offering made by My people Israel?' "Therefore the Lord, the God of Israel, declares: 'I promised that your house and your father's house would minister before me forever.' But now the Lord declares: 'Far be it from Me! Those who honor Me I will honor, but those who despise Me will be disdained. The time is coming when I will cut short your strength and the strength of your father's house, so that there will not be an old man in your family line and you will see distress in My dwelling. Although good will be done to Israel, in your family line there will never be an old man. Every one of you that I do not cut off from My altar will be spared only to blind your eyes with tears and to grieve your heart, and all your descendants will die in the prime of life. And what happens to your two sons, Hophni and Phinehas, will be a sign to you—they will both die on the same day. I will raise up for Myself a faithful priest, who will do according to what is in my heart and mind. I will firmly establish his house, and he will minister before My anointed one always (1 Samuel 2:22-35).

The first fulfillment *or immediate application of this prophesy:* Eli and his sons died and Samuel became the priest, the leader, kingmaker of Israel and the prophet in their place.

The second fulfillment: *"So Solomon removed Abiathar from the priesthood of the Lord, fulfilling the word the Lord had spoken at Shiloh about the house of Eli. The king put Benaiah son of Jehoiada over the army in Joab's position and replaced Abiathar with Zadok the priest"* (1 Kings 2:27,35). The priesthood passed completely from Eli's line when King Solomon removed Abiathar, a descendant of Eli and replaced him with Zadok.

The third fulfillment: *"So Christ also did not take upon himself the glory of becoming a high priest. But God said to him, 'You are my Son; today I have become your Father.' And he says in another place, 'You are a priest forever, in the order of Melchizedek'"* (Hebrews 5:5-6). The prophecy was ultimately fulfilled in Jesus Christ, the Messiah. He was the ultimate faithful priest, combining the priesthood and kingship together forever. Jesus was of the tribe of Judah.

Multiple application of the meaning of dreams is akin to multiple applicability of prophetic message. We can see this in a prophetic act performed by the prophet Zechariah in Zechariah 11:7-17. In this passage, Zechariah plays the role of the good shepherd who is rejected, an image Jesus would later apply to Himself. This also happens frequently in our dreams.

> So I pastured the flock marked for slaughter, particularly the oppressed of the flock. Then I took two staffs and called one Favour and the other Union, and I pastured the flock. In one month I got rid of the three shepherds. The flock detested me, and I grew weary of them and said, "I will not be your shepherd. Let the dying die, and the perishing perish. Let those who are left eat one another's flesh." Then I took my staff called Favour and broke it, revoking the covenant I had made with all the nations. It was revoked on that day, and so the afflicted of the flock who were watching me knew it was the word of the Lord. I told them, "If you think it best, give me my pay; but if not, keep it." So they paid me thirty pieces of silver. And the Lord said to me, "Throw it to the potter"—the handsome price at which they priced me! So I took the thirty pieces of silver and threw them into the house of the Lord to the potter. Then I broke my second staff called Union, breaking the brotherhood between Judah and Israel. Then the Lord said to me, "Take again the equipment of a foolish shepherd. For I am going to raise up a shepherd over the land who will not care for the lost, or seek the young, or heal the injured, or feed the healthy, but will eat the meat of the choice sheep, tearing off their hoofs. "Woe to the worthless shepherd, who deserts the flock! May the sword strike his arm and his right eye! May his arm be completely withered, his right eye totally blinded!" (Zechariah 11:7-17).

RECOGNIZING PROGRESSIVE REVELATION IN DREAM COMMUNICATIONS

God never reveals the totality of His heart's plan in a single message or dream. God reveals things to us in a progressive manner, in ways that we can handle at that moment.

Progressive revelation in dreams and visions can occur in any of the following ways:

- Further revelation on the subject.
- Emphasis on another aspect of the subject.
- New direction on the matter.
- Confirmation on the subject or part of the subject already revealed.
- Revealing further progression in relation to the roles of other people on the subject.
- Further progressive revelations through other people, circumstances, or events.

It is important to realize that some dreams that might appear as repeat dreams could in fact be progressive revelations on the discourse already begun with God in previous dreams. Realizing this, of course, will help the dreamer pay attention to the correct area.

Let us look at instances of progressive revelations in the Bible.

God revealed His intension to Abraham in a progressive manner.

Abraham's first revelation to leave his father's house and move to the land God would show him did not come with much detail: *"The Lord had said to Abram, 'Leave your country, your people and your father's household and go to the land I will show you. I will make you into a great nation and I will bless you; I will make your name great, and you will be a blessing. I will bless those who bless you, and whoever curses you I will curse; and all peoples on earth will be blessed through you.' So Abram left, as the Lord had told him; and Lot went with him. Abram was seventy-five years old when he set out from Haran"* (Gen. 12:1-4).

But despite God's economy of words to Abraham, he obeyed God. *"He took his wife Sarai, his nephew Lot, all the possessions they had accumulated and the people they had acquired in Haran, and they set out for the land of Canaan, and they arrived there. Abram traveled through the land as far as the site of the great tree of Moreh at Shechem. At that time the Canaanites were in the land"* (Gen. 12:5-6).

Then God furthered His explanation on the subject to Abraham on a later date. *"The Lord appeared to Abram and said, "To your offspring I will give this land." So he built an altar there to the Lord, who had appeared to him. From there he went on toward the hills east of Bethel and pitched his tent, with Bethel on the west and Ai on the east. There he built an altar to the Lord and called on the name of the Lord"* (Gen. 12:7-8).

God also showed a progressive pattern of His revelation to the prophet Daniel.

Daniel dreamt of the four beasts. In this dream, the four empires—Babylon, Medo-Persia, Greece, Rome—were symbolized by the brute force of the various animals: *lion; bear; leopard; and a beast.* In the dream of the four beasts, the emphasis was on the details of the Babylonian and Roman empires *though all four kingdoms were in the dream.*

Daniel also dreamt of a ram and goat. In this dream, Medo-Persia and Greece are symbolized by a ram and goat. God progressed further to give details of the Medo-Persia and Greek empires.

The apostle Paul also received revelations in a progressive manner.

Apostle Paul warned the sailors: *"Much time had been lost, and sailing had already become dangerous because by now it was after the Fast. So Paul warned them, 'Men, I can see that our voyage is going to be disastrous and bring great loss to ship and cargo, and to our own lives also.' But the centurion, instead of listening to what Paul said, followed the advice of the pilot and of the owner of the ship"* (Acts 27:9-11).

Later God gave further revelation on the matter to Paul: *"After the men had gone a long time without food, Paul stood up before them and said: 'Men, you should have taken my advice not to sail from Crete; then you would have spared yourselves this damage and loss. But now I urge you to keep up your courage, because not one of you will be lost; only the ship will be destroyed.* **Last night an angel of the God whose I am and whom I serve stood beside me and said, "Do not be afraid, Paul. You must stand trial before Caesar; and God has graciously given you the lives of all who sail with you." So keep up your courage, men, for I have faith in God that it will happen just as He told me.** *Nevertheless, we must run aground on some island'"* (Acts 27:21-26).

God's Purposes in Dreams and Visions

Ultimately, God uses dreams to align our hearts, thoughts, and intentions to His eternal purpose. He may use dreams in a variety of ways: to answer our questions; to appoint us to a new mission; to command changes in how we live; to commune with us concerning secrets of His heart; to promise us something yet to come; to teach us vital truths that we might have missed, and so forth.

Many misconceptions about dreams result from precepts of worldly wisdom. Humanistic ideology states that dreams only tell us unresolved aspects of a dreamer, such as anxieties, bitterness, jealousy, unforgiveness, secret yearnings, and untapped ambitions. This school of thought further claims that all these occur in dreams because the person has not recognized them while awake, or is perhaps even unwilling to admit to them. The fact is that God relates these aspects in our dreams both to correct our excesses and to guide us into truth. He brings them into our dreams for the purpose of aligning us with His eternal purpose.

Dreams have the power to expand, confirm, enlighten, enrich, and deepen your understanding of God's Word:

- Through dreams, we get more details and specific direction for achieving a given task. Dreams can also give hidden insight of wisdom specific to the situation.

- It is important to know that God does not send dreams to embarrass, condemn, or confuse us.

- Through dreams and visions, God grants us insightful understanding of our own hearts. The apostle Peter's wrong mindset that Gentiles were unclean (which came from his Jewish upbringing) was revealed to him through visions he received from God:

- God uses dreams and visions to give us insight into circumstances of life and the true reason behind our experiences. Abraham's dream of his descendants going into slavery in Egypt was foretold and explained as follows:

- God exposes satan's plans and gives us insight into hell's assignments.

For more information see *Dreams and Visions Volume 1* by Dr. Joe Ibojie

POINTS TO PONDER

1. The dynamics of how dreams are released to the mind from your spirit is enhanced by your faith in God. Without faith, revelations remain dormant. Once a revelation is processed in your mind, proper comprehension and correlation to your circumstance is influenced by the peace and godly liberty you enjoy. Have you found this to be true in your personal life?

    _____

    _____

2. The first and most important response to a revelation, is to pray for all the elements, events, and persons (friends and perceived enemies) that play a part in the revelation—do this even before you gain an understanding of the meaning of the revelation. Do you remember to pray first?

    _____

    _____

3. It is important to realize that some dreams that might appear as repeat dreams could in fact be progressive revelations on the discourse already begun with God in previous dreams. Realizing this will help you pay attention to the correct area. Have you had repeat dreams?

    _____

    _____

Chapter 4

REMEMBERING YOUR DREAMS AND DREAM REVELATIONS

IT IS IMPORTANT that we are able to recall or remember our dreams so that we might benefit from the wisdom in them. Our ability to receive, remember, understand, and apply our dreams—otherwise known as "dream life"—is not quite as passive as many tend to believe. As a matter of fact, everyone is capable of remembering his dreams or even developing an active dream life. However, many people may not realize that this is something they can attain. It is true that every (true) dream or vision is initiated by God, and we can position ourselves where God can talk to us in dreams. Also, once God has started dream discourse, we can take the discussion further by appropriately responding to what God might have shown us in the dream.

I believe the first place to start in the art of remembering our dreams is by paying attention to the seemingly insignificant things like having adequate physical rest, maintaining a peaceful living, and reducing the busyness of the routine of life. More often than not, these simple steps can reverse the failing ability to remember dreams. Reversing the failing ability to remember dreams is essential if one is to continue to hear God through dreams and visions. All over the world, a growing number of people experience diminishing ability to recall their dreams. This is a large category people. As I travel across the nations, I encounter countless number of people who fall into this category. In general, as we grows older, this problem inevitably confronts us as part of the aging process. What I believe we should do is apply basic principles of life and patiently work our way back to things we used to do that might have slipped during the challenges of the aging process.

Over the years, I have found that the following are some of the issues that may constitute hindrances to receiving and remembering dreams: *busyness of life, lack of peace, not meditating on the Word of God, lack of prayerfulness, and not paying attention to the first few minutes of waking up.* In particular it is worth noting that the first few minutes of waking up are when dreams are transmitted from the spirit of the dreamer to his mind. Remembrance takes place in the memory part of the human mind and therefore dreams can be lost or recaptured in the first few minutes of waking up.

The following steps are important and have helped me in my efforts to recover lost ground in the art of remembering dreams. They include:

- Peace in God; the measure of peace we enjoy determines the height of our spiritual experience in God.

- Quiet time with God; the more time we spend with God, the less we depend on our emotions, will, and mind. Adequate physical rest is important as a tired body often leaks anointing.

- Giving abundant worship to God, as worshiping God brings down His glory.

- Appropriate response to dreams; one of the main values of dreams is for us to align to the agenda of God and appropriate response will therefore allow God to further His discourse with us by giving more revelations.

- Obedience to the will of God is important; as the Bible says, "His will be done on earth as it is in heaven."

- Faithfulness in tithes and offerings; even God Himself said test Him on this and see if He will not open the windows of heaven (see Mal. 3:10).

- Dwelling in the richness of the eternal Word of God.

In addition to these seven factors, the following specific steps are important if we are to continue to remember or recall our dreams.

Reverse any form of spiritual drifting: Spiritual drifting is the quiet, gradual, slow, blind, and unintentional slipping away from the values of Christianity. All the efforts that I have taken in reversing areas of spiritual drifting, whether small or big, have always turned out to be very valuable. The first step I will usually take is to go back to doing the things I used to do that might have slipped away inadvertently. The writer of Hebrews admonished us that *"We must pay more careful attention, therefore, to what we have heard, so that we do not drift away"* (Heb. 2:1).

Spiritual drifting away from the standards of God is very common. But the most important thing is to realize it and repent and go back to God. The danger of spiritual drifting is the subtlety with which it creeps into the life of its victims. When people drift, they drift downward. No one drifts upward. To move upward is a premeditated process. Spiritual drifting is a common cause of not hearing from God, especially through dreams and visions, and is also a common cause of the fall of many anointed servants of God if not checked.

Develop a good listening art: Most people are simply not good at listening and so are not able hear properly from God or discern things happening in the super-natural realm. The art of hearing God begins with the ability to listen in the spirit. We must learn to quiet ourselves in the stillness of His peace. This then enables us to hear His still small voice. With this comes a better ability to hear Him including most other ways of divine communications other than dreams and visions.

Increase time spent in studying the Word of God and the time spent in fellow-shipping with God.

Prayerfulness and readiness to give God unreserved worship.

Faithfulness with your tithes/offerings. Remember, according to the Book of Malachi, God is obliged to open the window of heaven over us. Whenever the window of heaven is opened not only does material blessing come down but abundant revelations also come.

Be obedient to whatever God might have said to you.

Ask God specifically to reactivate your dream life and be detailed about it; as the Book of James puts it, *"we have not, because we ask not."*

In addition, the following are important, practical steps that are often neglected:

- Get a pen and dream journal and record your dreams no matter how scanty they may come; God rewards those who diligently seek Him. Handle with wisdom dreams that are only remembered in fragments!

- When you awake from spiritual encounters, calm yourself in the spirit for this enhances the process of remembering.

- Ask the Holy Spirit to remind you of the night's encounters.

- Try to recall the dreams of the night immediately after waking up, and then re-run the events as you have seen them in the dream, recalling as many details as your mind can remember. This process helps to transcribe the dream to the more durable ink of the memory.

- Write down whatever you remember, even if in fragments. Again, treat dreams remembered in fragments with caution, because they might be missing vital parts.

- Do not start to interpret a dream until you have finished writing down the dream, otherwise you may lose vital parts of the later scenes of the dream in the process.

- Pray about every thing or people you have seen in the dream or vision, whether friends or perceived enemies, bearing in mind that most events, people, and things in dreams are symbolic.

- Ask the Holy Spirit to give you clues for understanding your dreams.

DREAMS ARE LIKE STORIES TOLD IN PARABLES

One can say most dreams are like stories told in parables. God the Father speaks in riddles and parables, which include the parables of the night seasons. In the Book of Hosea, God says, *"I spoke to the prophets, gave them many visions and told parables through them"* (Hosea 12:10). Our Lord Jesus Christ also spoke in parables when He walked the earth: *"With many such parables [Jesus] spoke the Word to them, as they were to able bear and to comprehend and understand. **He did not tell them anything without a parable; but privately to His disciples** (those who were peculiarly His own) He explained everything [fully]"* (Mark 4:33-34 AMP).

Parables are like wrapped gifts and you may have to dig deep to appreciate the value of the gift. Some people may find the packaging of a wrapped gift acceptable and others may find it distractive. Only those who diligently unpacked the wrapping will find the value of the truth hidden within. There is a heart connection in dreams as the Book of Numbers describes, *"Then He said; Hear My words! If there is a prophet among you, I, the Lord, make Myself known* [the awareness of the nature of God revealed] *to him in a vision. I speak to him* [further deepening of understanding welded into the heart of the dreamer] *in a dream"* (Num. 12:6). As a result, there is a close-knit relationship between the heart of the dreamer, the Spirit of God, and the understanding of the parables in dream messages.

Parables become unfolded and are easy to understand when the truth is supernaturally revealed to the heart yielded to God, a heart not hardened by unrighteousness. The Pharisees took offence at Jesus when He taught in parables because their hearts were hard and therefore dull spiritually; they were unable to understand the parables in His teaching. Speaking on the subject of lack of understanding and the hardening of hearts, Paul says to the Ephesians, *"They are darkened in their understanding and separated from the life of God because of the ignorance that is in them due to the hardening of their hearts* (Eph. 4:18). Consequently, without the help of the Holy Spirit, no person can understand the parables in dreams and visions. Perhaps this is why most people give up too easily in their dependence on human effort to gain understanding of dreams. But the Bible says, *"It is the glory of God to conceal a matter. But the glory of the kings is to search out a matter"* (Prov. 25:2).

Also, this unique heart connection enables the dreamer to recognize correct interpretation as well as ensure that the dreamer does not become too easily deceived by bogus and untrue interpretation. No person can help the dreamer to gain understanding of his or her dreams unless the Holy Spirit allows the interpreter into this *close-knit relationship* between the dreamer and God. Likewise, no one should argue with the dreamer as to the meaning of a dream, because when an interpretation is correct, there is a birthing in the spirit of the dreamer that bears witness or resonates in the dreamer that the interpretation is correct. This inner witness illuminates the mind of the dreamer. Divinely inspired interpretation has enough power to break any erroneous mindset.

The inescapable inference must be that there exists a form of divine "sealing" (or covering or the folding) of the understanding of God's parables. This sealing ensures that only those for whom the parables are intended receive the true understanding of the secrets inherent in the parables, even though everyone may hear them.

Somehow, the understanding of these parables, or more specifically the parables in dreams, is connected to the state of the heart of the person, whether or not the person's heart is yielded to God. For those whose hearts are yielded to Jesus Christ, they are able to commune with the indwelling Holy Spirit who then unfolds the meaning of the parable to them. As the Bible says, *"...when He was alone with His disciples, He explained everything"* (Mark 4:33-34).

And when Jesus Christ left the earth, He did not leave us as orphans: ***"I will not leave you as orphans..."*** (John 14:18); and then He also says, *"I have much more to say to you, more than you can now bear. But when He,* **the Spirit of truth, comes, He will guide you into all truth.** *He will not speak on His own; He will speak only what He hears, and He will tell you what is yet to come"* (John 16:12-13). To date, Jesus Christ continues to explain the meaning of divine parables of God to us through the Holy Spirit, so that the secrets of the mysteries of God's Kingdom will be preserved for those who are heirs of the salvation. *"The disciples came to him and asked, 'Why do you speak to the people in parables?' He replied, 'The knowledge of the secrets of the kingdom of heaven has been given to you, but not to them'"* (Matt. 13:10-11).

Jesus Christ further explained to the disciples why everybody might hear His parable teachings but only to His disciples did He explain them. In a way, this is like saying that anyone can receive dreams, but only those whose hearts are yielded to God will understand them: *"And He said to them. To you has been entrusted the mystery of the kingdom of God, [that is, the secret counsels of God which are hidden from the ungodly]; but for those out side [of our circle] everything becomes a parable. In order that they may [indeed] look and look but not see and perceive, and may hear and hear but not grasp and comprehend..."* (Mark 4:11-12 AMP).

Perhaps this is also why Pharaoh of Egypt and Nebuchadnezzar of Babylon recognized the correct interpretations of their dreams when they heard them. Also because of this close-knit relationship between the dreamer and God, the Egyptian and Babylonian magicians, astrologers, and the wise men were unable to gain the understanding of the dreams the kings told them, *because God did not give them that understanding.*

I, Nebuchadnezzar, was at home in my palace, contented and prosperous. I had a dream that made me afraid. As I was lying in my bed, the images and visions that passed through my mind terrified me. So I *commanded that all the wise men of Babylon be brought before me to interpret the dream for me. When the magicians, enchanters, astrologers and diviners came, I told them the dream, **but they could not interpret it for me**. Finally, Daniel came into my presence and I told him the dream. (He is called Belteshazzar, after the name of my god, and the spirit of the holy gods is in him.)* (Daniel 4:4-8).

*In the morning his mind was troubled, so he sent for all the magicians and wise men of Egypt. Pharaoh told them his dreams, **but no one could interpret them for him*** (Genesis 41:8).

King Nebuchadnezzar attested to the fact that Daniel was able to interpret the dreams not because of his intelligence but because *"the spirit of the holy gods is in you."* *"This is the dream that I, King Nebuchadnezzar, had. Now, Belteshazzar, tell me what it means, for none of the wise men in my kingdom can interpret it for me. **But you can, because the spirit of the holy gods is in you"*** (Dan. 4:18). What King Nebuchadnezzar unknowingly called the holy gods is the Spirit of God that came upon Daniel, the interpreter, and helped him with the interpretation.

In Egypt, this is what Joseph said regarding the interpretation of dreams: *"Pharaoh said to Joseph, 'I had a dream, and no one can interpret it. But I have heard it said of you that when you hear a dream you can interpret it.' 'I cannot do it,' Joseph replied to Pharaoh, 'but **God will give Pharaoh the answer he desires'"*** (Gen. 41:15-16). Earlier when speaking to the cup bearer and the baker in an Egyptian dungeon, Joseph said, *"...**Do not interpretations belong to God**? Tell me your dreams"* (Gen. 40:8).

This is my conclusion, *if interpretation belongs to God, no one can get it unless God gives it to him.*

HOW TO HANDLE DREAM REVELATIONS

Revelation is God's disclosure of Himself and His truth or "a manifestation of divine will or truth"[1] or simply "a divine communication."[2] Throughout this book the term *revelation* is seen in this context, and does not include information. *Information* is knowledge derived from study or experience. There are many ways through which we can receive revelations from God. Paramount in the ways we receive is the pivotal role of the Word of God. By studying the Word of God, one can get revelation as the prophet Daniel experienced:

> *In the first year of Darius son of Ahasuerus (a Mede by descent), who was made ruler over the Babylonian kingdom—in the first year of his reign, I, Daniel, understood from the Scriptures, according to the word of the Lord given to Jeremiah the prophet, that the desolation of Jerusalem would last seventy years* (Daniel 9:1-2).

In addition to studying the Word of God, other ways to receive revelation include dreams and visions. Whatever way we receive revelations, the way we handle them is important. The advice that emanated from the divine wisdom endowed to King Solomon by the Holy Spirit did not benefit him especially in the later part of his life. He failed to handle those later-life events according to the principles embodied in the wisdom of God. For every one of us, the way we handle our dreams and visions will influence and determine whether we fulfill our destiny or not. Pastor and author Myles Munroe said that the richest place in the world is not the bank, but the graveyard home and final resting place of man's physical existence because many people fail to handle and respond appropriately to their God-given dreams and aspirations and died with unfulfilled dreams.

The reception of a revelation does not necessarily guarantee the recipient with all the benefits inherent in the revelation, and it is only with proper handling of what is received that one can maximize the benefits that are in the revelation. King Solomon was one of the greatest and wisest leaders the world has ever known, but he slid into failure, selfishness, and overindulgence despite the wisdom of God that came through him to whole world. Ultimately he failed to please God with his life, simply because he consistently failed to follow or respond appropriately to the wisdom in his revelations on a personal level.

> *God gave Solomon wisdom and very great insight, and a breadth of understanding as measureless as the sand on the seashore. Solomon's wisdom was greater than the wisdom of all the men of the East, and greater than all the wisdom of Egypt. He was wiser than any other man, including Ethan the Ezrahite—wiser than Heman, Calcol and Darda, the sons of Mahol. And his fame spread to all the surrounding*

nations. He spoke three thousand proverbs and his songs numbered a thousand and five. He described plant life, from the cedar of Lebanon to the hyssop that grows out of walls. He also taught about animals and birds, reptiles and fish. Men of all nations came to listen to Solomon's wisdom, sent by all the kings of the world, who had heard of his wisdom (1 Kings 4:29-34).

Despite Solomon's great wisdom, the Bible describes in First Kings what became of King Solomon in his later days.

King Solomon, however, loved many foreign women besides Pharaoh's daughter—Moabites, Ammonites, Edomites, Sidonians and Hittites. They were from nations about which the Lord had told the Israelites, "You must not intermarry with them, because they will surely turn your hearts after their gods." Nevertheless, Solomon held fast to them in love. He had seven hundred wives of royal birth and three hundred concubines, and his wives led him astray. As Solomon grew old, his wives turned his heart after other gods, and his heart was not fully devoted to the Lord his God, as the heart of David his father had been. He followed Ashtoreth the goddess of the Sidonians, and Molech the detestable god of the Ammonites. So Solomon did evil in the eyes of the Lord; he did not follow the Lord completely, as David his father had done (1 Kings 11:1-6).

Solomon did not handle his own revelations appropriately and therefore failed to benefit from the wisdom inherent in his revelations.

The followings are some of the ways people handled their dreams and visions in the Bible.

Pondering.

Pondering is the process of weighing something in the mind or giving due consideration to something. This is the least way we should react to a dream or vision. I am often amazed to see how most people fail to ponder on what they receive from God. Pondering opens up the person to countless possibilities, brings understanding, and also draws attention to the majesty of God. The following people were noted in the Bible as having pondered on what they had received from God.

- *"While **Peter thought about the vision**, the Spirit said to him, 'Behold three men are seeking you. Arise therefore, go down and go with them, doubting nothing; for I have sent them'"* (Acts 10:19).

- **Jacob** pondered what Joseph's dreams meant. *"This time he told his father as well as his brothers; but his father rebuked him. What is this? He asked. Shall I indeed, and your mother and brothers come and bow before you? His brothers were fit to be tied concerning this affairs, but his father gave it quit a bit of thought and wondered what it all meant!"* (Gen. 37:10-11 TLB).

- **Mary** the mother of Jesus pondered or treasured what she heard in her heart: *"Then He went down to Nazareth with them and was obedient to them. But His mother treasured all these things in her heart"* (Luke 2:51).

Again, the least anybody can do when God gives one a dream is to ponder on the dream.

Moving in proportion to your faith.

Gideon was encouraged and gained confidence to lead the Israelites to war by a dream and its interpretation that he overheard during divinely inspired espionage to the Midianite camp. At first Gideon lacked the faith to lead the people, but God asked him to go on espionage to enemy's camp. When he overhead a dream and its interpretation, he gained confidence to carry out what God commanded him to do. Gideon moved in proportion to his faith and obtained resounding victory.

> *During that night the Lord said to Gideon, "Get up, go down against the camp, because I am going to give it into your hands. If you are afraid to attack, go down to the camp with your servant Purah and listen to what they are saying. Afterward, you will be encouraged to attack the camp." So he and Purah his servant went down to the outposts of the camp. The Midianites, the Amalekites and all the other eastern peoples had settled in the valley, thick as locusts. Their camels could no*

more be counted than the sand on the seashore. Gideon arrived just as a man was telling a friend his dream. "I had a dream," he was saying. "A round loaf of barley bread came tumbling into the Midianite camp. It struck the tent with such force that the tent overturned and collapsed." His friend responded, "This can be nothing other than the sword of Gideon son of Joash, the Israelite. God has given the Midianites and the whole camp into his hands." When Gideon heard the dream and its interpretation, he worshiped God. He returned to the camp of Israel and called out, "Get up! The Lord has given the Midianite camp into your hands." Dividing the three hundred men into three companies, he placed trumpets and empty jars in the hands of all of them, with torches inside (Judges 7:9-16).

Notice Gideon did not move until he attained the required level of faith. Without faith, it is impossible to please God.

Handle whatever you receive truthfully.

King Abimelech was warned in a dream to return Sarah, Abraham's wife, to Abraham. When he discovered the truth that Sarah was the wife of Abraham, he truthfully returned her to her husband and made the appropriate absolution (see Gen. 20).

Be alert and sensitive in the spirit.

Apostle Peter did not immediately gain the understanding of the meaning of his vision, but as he pondered on it he remained alert and sensitive in the spirit, then the understanding unfolded to him in stages (see Acts 10:9-48).

Be humble enough to know when to seek help to understand dreams.

Even though the prophets Zechariah and Daniel were seasoned dreamers, they were both humble enough to ask the "angel interpreter" for the meaning of the many scenes in their dreams that they did not understand. Of the prophet Zechariah the Bible says, *"I asked the angel who talked with me, 'What are these, my lord?' He answered, 'Do you not know what these are?' 'No, my lord,' I replied. So he said to me, 'This is the word of the Lord to Zerubbabel: "Not by might nor by power, but by My Spirit," says the Lord Almighty. 'What are you, O mighty mountain? Before Zerubbabel you will become level ground. Then he will bring out the capstone to shouts of "God bless it! God bless it!"'"* (Zech. 4:4-7).

And of Daniel we read, *"I, Daniel, was troubled in spirit, and the visions that passed through my mind disturbed me. I approached one of those standing there and asked him the true meaning of all this. So he told me and gave me the interpretation of these things"* (Dan. 7:15).

Also, Pharaoh and Nebuchadnezzar sought the meaning of their dreams. Though Pharaoh and Nebuchadnezzar were powerful kings in their days, they were humble enough to seek the meaning of their dreams. *"Pharaoh said to Joseph, 'I had a dream, and no one can interpret it. But I have heard it said of you that when you hear a dream you can interpret it.' 'I cannot do it,' Joseph replied to Pharaoh, 'but God will give Pharaoh the answer he desires'"* (Gen. 41:15-16). And in Babylon, Nebuchadnezzar says, *"Belteshazzar, chief of the magicians, I know that the spirit of the holy gods is in you, and no mystery is too difficult for you. Here is my dream; interpret it for me"* (Dan. 4:9).

In the Book of Genesis 41:17-24, the Bible gives the details of the dream that Pharaoh had. The account of Pharaoh's correct handling of the dreams involved the followings steps:

- He recalled the dreams.
- He pondered on the dreams.
- He went a great length to seek the meaning of the dreams.

Pharaoh received the dream meaning from a Hebrew captive in Babylon. This account is recorded in Genesis 41:25-32, and from it we can learn the following lessons:

- Pharaoh was prepared and humble enough to listen to his subjects.
- Pharaoh's narration of the dreams to Joseph contained more details than he previously told the magicians and wise men which shows he had pondered further on the dreams and gained more insights between when he first told the wise men of Egypt and when he told Joseph, the Hebrew: *"Then behold, seven other cows came up after them, poor and*

very ugly and gaunt, such ugliness as I have never seen in all the land of Egypt" (Gen. 41:19). Later Pharaoh says, *"When they had eaten them up, no one would have know that they had eaten them for they were just as ugly as at the beginning. So I awoke"* (Gen. 41:21).

- When we pay attention to our dreams, we will find their fuller meaning unfolds with time.

- Joseph gave Pharaoh the correct interpretation.

- Pharaoh recognized the correct interpretation because the interpretation resonated with his spirit.

In Genesis 41:33-40 Joseph gave Pharaoh a word of wisdom and the way forward.

- Pharaoh and his officials recognized the good counsel in Joseph's interpretation.

- Pharaoh assumed responsibility for what was revealed to him.

- Pharaoh put Joseph in charge of the plans he suggested.

The benefits of this correct handling by Pharaoh of his dreams were outstanding; *"The seven years of abundance in Egypt came to an end, and the seven years of famine began, just as Joseph had said. There was famine in all the other lands, but in the whole land of Egypt there was food. When all Egypt began to feel the famine, the people cried to Pharaoh for food. Then Pharaoh told all the Egyptians, 'Go to Joseph and do what he tells you.' When the famine had spread over the whole country, Joseph opened the storehouses and sold grain to the Egyptians, for the famine was severe throughout Egypt. And all the countries came to Egypt to buy grain from Joseph, because the famine was severe in all the world'"* (Gen. 41:53-57).

Handle revelations rightly, not poorly.

On the other hand, King Nebuchadnezzar handled poorly one of the dreams he had. This story is recorded in Daniel 4:10-17. Though he recalled his dream, pondered on it, and sought the meaning, his response to the interpretation given to him was very poor. Daniel, a Jewish captive gave him the interpretation and advised him: *"Therefore, O king, be pleased to accept my advice: Renounce your sins by doing what is right, and your wickedness by being kind to the oppressed. It may be that then your prosperity will continue"* (Dan. 4:27).

Sadly the Bible records that *"he did not heed the advice."* Eventually the dream was fulfilled and the calamity came upon King Nebuchadnezzar.

> *All this happened to King Nebuchadnezzar. Twelve months later, as the king was walking on the roof of the royal palace of Babylon, he said, "Is not this the great Babylon I have built as the royal residence, by my mighty power and for the glory of my majesty?" The words were still on his lips when a voice came from heaven, "This is what is decreed for you, King Nebuchadnezzar: Your royal authority has been taken from you. You will be driven away from people and will live with the wild animals; you will eat grass like cattle. Seven times will pass by for you until you acknowledge that the Most High is sovereign over the kingdoms of men and gives them to anyone he wishes." Immediately what had been said about Nebuchadnezzar was fulfilled. He was driven away from people and ate grass like cattle. His body was drenched with the dew of heaven until his hair grew like the feathers of an eagle and his nails like the claws of a bird"* (Daniel 4:28-33).

Public pronouncement of the promises of God in one's life should only be for the building up of others and never for personal aggrandizement. Joseph mishandled his dreams and stirred up acrimony in his family. Even his father, Jacob was displeased; *"His brothers said to him, "Do you intend to reign over us? Will you actually rule us?" And they hated him all the more because of his dream and what he had said"* (Gen. 37:8). *"Then he had another dream, and he told it to his brothers. "Listen," he said, "I had another dream, and this time the sun and moon and eleven stars were bowing down to me"* (Gen. 37:9).

HANDLING A WARNING DREAM

There are four possible ways to handle a warning dream that we will explore.

1. ***Pray and take action to avert the danger*** like the prophet Amos did on behalf of Israel: *"This is what the Sovereign Lord showed me: He was*

preparing swarms of locusts after the king's share had been harvested and just as the second crop was coming up. When they had stripped the land clean, I cried out, 'Sovereign Lord, forgive! How can Jacob survive? He is so small!' So the Lord relented. 'This will not happen,' the Lord said. This is what the Sovereign Lord showed me: The Sovereign Lord was calling for judgment by fire; it dried up the great deep and devoured the land. Then I cried out, 'Sovereign Lord, I beg you, stop! How can Jacob survive? He is so small!' So the Lord relented. 'This will not happen either,' the Sovereign Lord said" (Amos 7:1-6). To pray and take action is the preferable option.

2. **Pray for divine wisdom to handle the situation; if the danger is not preventable,** pray to take advantage of the impending situation like Pharaoh did following the advice of Joseph the dream interpreter. *"The plan seemed good to Pharaoh and to all his officials. So Pharaoh asked them, 'Can we find anyone like this man, one in whom is the spirit of God?' Then Pharaoh said to Joseph, 'Since God has made all this known to you, there is no one so discerning and wise as you. You shall be in charge of my palace, and all my people are to submit to your orders. Only with respect to the throne will I be greater than you'"* (Gen. 41:37-40).

3. **Fail to heed the warning.** King Nebuchadnezzar did not heed the advice of Daniel and the calamity came upon him (see Dan. 4:24-37).

4. **Move opposite to the divine wisdom of the revelations.** Over the years, I have found that some people mishandle warning revelations and in the process hasten the pace of bringing to fulfillment what the revelation warns about. For instance, if God warns a dreamer of a relationship that is not going well, most dreamers, unless where inevitable, will withdraw from the person or from the relationship. But in majority of such cases, the heart of love requires the dreamer to first seek God's face for the appropriate response. Maybe bringing harmony to the troubled relationship is the appropriate reaction. Avoidance of the person may not necessarily be God's prescription for the occasion. The Bible says as much as it depends on us, we should be at peace with all people. From my experience, such avoidance almost invariably aggravates any misunderstanding bringing further acrimony.

ENDNOTES

1. Reader's Digest, Universal Dictionary (London: Reader Digest Association limited, 1987).

2. Concise English Dictionary (London: Tophi Books, 1990).

POINTS TO PONDER

1. Everyone is capable of remembering dreams and developing an active dream life. Every (true) dream or vision is initiated by God, and you can position yourself so God can talk to you in dreams. After God has started dream discourse, you can take the discussion further by appropriately responding to what He might have shown you in the dream. Are you willing to step out in faith to receive what He has to say to you during a dream? Take another step further and apply your revelation in a godly way!

2. Spiritual drifting is the quiet, gradual, slow, blind, and unintentional slipping away from the values of Christianity—it is very common. The danger of spiritual drifting is the subtlety with which it creeps into the life of its victims. When people drift, they drift downward. No one drifts upward. In what direction are you drifting?

3. Parables are like wrapped gifts and you may have to dig deep to appreciate the value of the gift. You may find the packaging acceptable or maybe distractive. Only those who diligently unpack the wrapping will find the value of the truth hidden within. Are you unwrapping your gift with eager expectancy?

Chapter 5

My Intimate Moments With God

IN THIS CHAPTER, I share some of the intimate moments of my dream experiences and how God has helped me in each situation. By sharing these experiences, I hope to help others who may have had somewhat similar experiences.

People in Dreams

People are often symbolic in dreams. Over the years, I have had the following scenes in my dreams and I have given their interpretation as they perhaps relate to me. Nothing is cast in iron, but in this chapter I have given what they commonly mean to me. However, everyone should rely on his own established pattern of communication with God, as our experiences may be different.

When a spiritual leader or a covering pastor appears in my dream:

- This appearance may simply be symbolic of what the person or what the church has imparted into my life.

- It may be a timely divine message, such as a similar anointing on the leader is coming on me.

- It may be a literal representation of the leader.

- Sometimes if in the dream the leader shows incongruous lack of spiritual strength not consistent with my perceived level of his actual spiritual standing, it may be symbolic of the fact that his impartation in my life is being poorly handled or is weakened by things in my life. It may also mean a call for intercession for the leader.

When an unfaithful friend appears in my dream:

- It may be a literal representation of the person.
- It may be me! Sometimes when God wants to show us that we also have some measure of unfaithfulness, measure of unfaithfulness we detest in the person, He will often use the friend as symbolic of the dreamer. First to indicate how repulsive He finds that little bit of the trait in us, and second to test the intent of our hearts, whether we will pray or intercede for the person, in which case we would actually be praying for ourselves.

SPIRITUAL WARFARE IN DREAMS

How the need to intensify spiritual warfare is indicated in my dream:

- Any appearance of military personnel
- A dream in which I walk into a military parade
- Warplanes
- Warships or rescue boats
- Warhorses or chariots
- Warfare

How the need to increase spiritual surveillance is indicated in my dream:

- Going on a hunting expedition
- Hunting for wild beasts
- Wearing a camouflage uniform

- Spy mission
- The scenes of post-war casualties; in particular this may indicate the need to restrategize to avoid casualties
- Sudden appearance of an enemy troops

How inadequate preparation for spiritual warfare is indicated in my dream:

- A dream in which I am part of a disorganized army
- Going to war without adequate weapons
- Going to war without adequate uniform
- Going to war without shoes or with inappropriate shoes
- Absence of back-up supplies in the midst of war
- Doors or windows in my house that are not securely closed
- Cracks in the walls
- Driving a poorly maintained army van
- Driving an army van with tires not fully inflated; lack of fullness of the power of the Holy Spirit

Fear and Indecision in Dreams

Practical tips about how I handle warning dreams include the following. Handling warning dreams in fear may hasten the chance of the warning actually coming to pass in real life. Once you are fearful, your prayers are without faith and therefore ineffective. Job says, *"what I feared has come upon me"* (Job 3:25). God once told me that if I genuinely believe that prayers have averted a "revealed danger," and heeded the advice given in the dream, the danger would not come. From my experience, it is safe to assume a prayer of faith can avert a revealed danger. First because God reveals to redeem; and second, if the danger is not averted, God is often obliged to repeat the warning. This has been my experience.

A scene of running from a perceived danger in a dream when other people seem unperturbed is usually indicative of an area of unfounded fear in my life. This sort of situation is equivalent to a false alarm kind of scenario.

In my experience, a scene of inability to locate a place or location that should otherwise be easy in my natural life circumstance often indicates an area of indecision or insecurity in my life. For instance, the inability to locate a bedroom in the house may suggest that the dreamer has areas of indecision, times of intense anxiety, or confusion that the Lord wants the dreamer to handle, decide, or be corrected by God if wrong, or approved if right. The implication is that God believes that the dreamer has enough background to make an informed and righteous decision. In other words, God is waiting for the dreamer to face the matter. As the Bible says in the Book of Isaiah, *"Whether you turn to the right or to the left, your ears will hear a voice behind you, saying, "This is the way; walk in it"* (Isa. 30:21). This is also a common feature of senile or premature senile memory impairment, so these kinds of dreams are common with elderly people.

CHILDREN IN DREAMS

In most of my dreams, my natural children are symbolic of the different aspects of my ministry or anointing. So over the time I have learned which of them commonly represent the prophetic, pastoral, and evangelistic anointing. This is along the principles that children are very precious gifts from God and they are as precious to us as God's gifting in our lives is to God. Also I have found that children in dreams indicate the actual gifting in the child. God's choice of symbols in our dreams is not haphazard but purposeful and directed to reveal what may not be immediately obvious to us.

CHILDHOOD DREAMS

Most memorable dreams from childhood are often recurring or have a recurring theme. As they are often repeated, they have a long lasting impression on the dreamer. They are indicative of what often constitutes the pattern of common life challenges to the dreamer. Dreams from childhood may help create spiritual preparedness that goes deeper than natural understanding can offer and act as a propeller during times of challenges. Childhood dreams impart into the dreamer a deep sense of destiny that would be hard to erase by life circumstances. Many people survive what others may not be able to withstand because in their spirit they carry divine destiny imparted to them from childhood by God!

Interpreting Other People's Dreams

The principles I recommend for interpreting other people's dreams follow. In interpreting for others, the interpreter should bear in mind:

- The value of the prophetic anointing in the art of interpreting other people's dreams cannot be overemphasized, because certain scenes in dreams can act as prophecy signals for the interpreter of dreams. A prophecy signal is what prompts or stirs up the prophetic anointing in a person.

- When interpreting for other people, the interpreter should avoid overbearing interpretations; they may interfere with the punch of God's intended message or wisdom.

- The interpreter should avoid being melancholic, this will help keep the dreamer from emotional backlash and help keep peace and joy alive in the dreamer even if the dream was a warning.

- The interpreter should view the dream's message from God's perspective, speak from the heart of God, keeping in mind that God is love and it is not His wish that any should perish but all should come to the knowledge of Him—be frank and truthful about it!

- Handle warning dreams with wisdom and always leave a person hopeful.

- Intimate with the dreamer, because most dreams are divine responses to the questions in the heart of the dreamer and so the interpreter needs to know the preoccupation in the mind of the dreamer.

- Interpret from the life the dreamer is familiar with; God will use what the dreamer is familiar with to explain what the dreamer may not yet know.

- Interpret symbols from the world the dreamer is familiar with; symbols may derive meaning from the dreamer's life experience.

HOW I RECOGNIZE TRUE AND FALSE DREAMS

The Bible speaks of dreams in two categories: those sent by God (true dreams or spiritual dreams) and false dreams not sent by God. This categorization is different from scientific or medical classification of dreams and visions. Scientific knowledge and understanding on the subject of dream is limited only to the dreaming process at the mind level. Therefore scientists may not appreciate or readily grasp the truth and wisdom of spiritual dreams. Knowledge and wisdom of psychology is limited to dreams occurring only at the mind level that fall into the category that the Bible refers to as false dreams. Without this appreciation, many may find it hard to understand how biblical perspectives of dreams and visions differ from the knowledge of dreams in medical science.

First, let us look at true dreams. Paula Price, in her book *The Prophet's Dictionary,* defines spiritual dreams as, *"A sleep dream that unfolds the activities of the invisible realm **using as its communications the normal language of the dreamer in the sleep.** The spiritual dream employs **the symbolism of the creation applied by Creator, God to His world.** Prophecies and prophetic visions are obtained this way. Spiritual dreams often need interpretation for the dreamer **to understand, act on and correctly apply their truth in daily affairs.** Spiritual dreams may be had by anyone. One does not need to be a prophet or prophetic to receive one as they are the communiqués of the invisible world to those on earth.*[1] This passage expresses key truths in dreams and dream life.

A true dream is a form of pictorial revelation received in the spirit when one is sleeping. It is transmitted to the mind immediately, the mind wakes up from sleep and it is in the mind that comprehension occurs. My conclusion: all true dreams pass through the spirit of the dreamer. Sleep is the temporary suspension of the power of the mind and the body. Therefore, commonly the power of the mind and the body do not directly participate in the reception of dreams.

Because true dreams are imparted to the spirit of the dreamer, when a dreamer strengthens his or her spirit, dream experience will also be enhanced. Let me explain how a person can strengthen his spirit man and what the functional components of human spirit are:

- The wisdom of God (the life application of the Word of God).

- The sanctified conscience, (the laying aside of personal agenda).
- Communion (the art of spending intimate and quality time with God).

By studying the Bible, spending time with God, and giving God worship, dream experiences will become robust. As a result of applying these components to your life, the influences from the soul realm—emotion, the mind, and the human will—will be reduced and the spirit man becomes better expressed.

On the other hand, false dreams are not spiritual dreams. In general, false dreams involve only the mind of the person; that is one of the reasons they are called non-spiritual dreams in that they do not involve nor pass through the person's spirit. Even God Himself gave a clear and unambiguous definition of false dreams and visions: *"Did you not see **a false vision** and speak a lying divination **when you said, 'The Lord declares,' but it is not I who have spoken?"** (Ezek. 13:7 NASB). In essence, if it is not Holy-Spirit initiated or inspired, it is false.

False dreams actually happen only at the mind level; and according Jeremiah 23, they occur principally in two ways. False dreams are either "made-up stories" or are "delusions of the mind" of the dreamer.

MADE-UP STORIES

> *"'Listen to the dream I had from God last night' they say. And then they proceed to lie in My name, how long will this continue? If they are 'prophets' they are prophets of deceit, inventing everything they say. By telling these false dreams they are trying to get My people to forget Me in the same way as their fathers did, who turned away to idols of Baal. Let these false prophets tell their dreams and let My true messengers faithfully proclaim My every word. There is a difference between chaff and wheat! Does not My word burn like fire? ...Is not it like a mighty hammer that smashes the rock to pieces? So I stand against these prophets who get their messages from each other, these smooth-tongued prophets who say 'This message is from God.' **Their made-up dreams are flagrant lies that lead My people into sins. I did not send them and they have no message at all for My people,"** says the Lord* (Jeremiah 23:25-32 TLB).

For thus says the Lord of hosts, the God of Israel: Do not let your prophets and your diviners who are in your midst deceive you, nor listen to **your dreams which you cause to be dreamed** (Jeremiah 29:8).

The Lord of heaven's armies, the God of Israel, says: "Do not let the false prophets and mediums that are there among you fool you. **Do not listen to the dreams that they invent,** *for they prophesy lies in My name. I have not sent them," says the Lord* (Jeremiah 29:8 TLB).

The phrase "your dreams which you cause to be dreamed" refers to dreams invented because of people pressuring their prophets to declare dreams—regardless of whether or not they actually had one. In the days of Jeremiah, prophets were sent on vision or dream quests and were expected to receive dreams or visions as evidence of their being true prophets. As a result, many made up stories merely to save face.

Then the Lord said to me "The prophets are prophesying lies in My name. I have not sent them or appointed them or spoken to them. They are prophesying to you **false visions,** *divination, idolatries and the* **delusions of their own minds** (Jeremiah 14:14).

Then the Lord said: "The prophets are telling lies in My name. I did not send them or tell them to speak or give them any message. **They prophesy visions and revelations they have never seen nor heard;** *they speak foolishness concocted out of their own lying hearts* (Jeremiah 14:14 TLB).

Then the Lord said to me, "the [false] prophets prophesied lies in My name. I send them not, neither have I commanded them, nor have I spoken to them. They prophesied to you **a false or pretended vision,** *a worthless divination, [conjuring or practicing magic, trying to call forth the responses supposed to be given by idols], and the deceit of their own minds* (Jeremiah 14:14 AMP).

Also, in the Book of Ezekiel, God spoke about the false dreams and visions: *"And her prophets have daubed them over with whitewash, seeing false visions and divining lies to them, saying "Thus says the Lord God—when the Lord has not spoken"* (Ezek. 22:28 AMP).

> *Son of man, prophecy against the prophets of Israel who prophecy; and say to those who prophesy out of their own mind and heart: Hear the word of the Lord! Thus says the Lord God: Woe to the foolish prophets who follow their own spirit [things they have not seen] and have seen nothing"* (Ezekiel 13:2-3 AMP).

> *Ask the Lord for rain in the springtime, it is the Lord who makes the storm clouds. He gives showers of rain to men, and plants of the field to everyone. **The idols speak deceit, dreamers see visions that lie. They tell dreams that are false.** They give comfort in vain. Therefore the people wander like sheep oppressed for lack of a shepherd* (Zechariah 10:1-2).

DELUSIONS OF THE MIND

There are various subcategories of the delusions of the mind: *"I have heard what the prophets say who prophesy lies in My name. They say 'I had a dream! I had a dream!' How long will this continue in the hearts of these lying prophets, **who prophesy the delusions of their own minds?"*** (Jer. 23:25-26).

Also, various forms of delusions of the mind can follow the use and misuse of drugs, alcohol, or the use of other dangerous substances. A notable form of the delusion of the mind is called *hallucination*.

Hallucination is a form of false dreams. It is the false perception with a compelling sense of the reality of something not really present. It does not involve the spirit of the person. It is an infringement of the mind. Many conditions or chemicals can induce hallucinations. These include drugs, anaesthesia, chemical imbalance, illicit drug usage or addiction, alcoholism, mental disorders, or hormonal imbalance. Hallucination is false perception, therefore belongs in the category of false dreams.

Mild hallucinations occur commonly but only become easily perceived during sleep, when the influences or the natural noise of the mind, the intellect, and the busyness of the body are at their minimized state. Hence mild hallucinations often appear as dreams of the night or sleep. On the other hand, severe forms of hallucination, as may occur in mental disorders, are less common, but can manifest whether the person is asleep or awake.

I believe what is critically important is to be able to differentiate true dreams from false dreams on a personal level. In true dreams and visions, God utilizes very individualistic forms in communicating with the person in dreams. These individualistic forms are usually taken from life experiences, biblical examples, and personal traits and attributes that are specific to the dreamer. Therefore correct, and proper interpretation must come from the dreamer because of the individualistic traits. True meaning of dreams can only be achieved by examining the prevailing setting of the dreamer; this is the framework that God uses to give crucial messages. Prevailing circumstances in the dreamer's life often play up in the dream's drama.

On the other hand, false dreams and visions are often bizarre or a haphazard gathering of events or occurrences.

Key distinguishing features of false dreams or visions:

- Often bizarre and haphazard gathering of events or occurrences.
- No logical trend, no real discernable storyline or plot.
- No correlation with other dreams of the dreamer.
- Often fragmented or disjointed.
- Does not correlate with the Word of God.
- Usually no wisdom is noticeable.
- Often leaves the person empty and drained.
- Leaves the person in fear and in confusion.

Another characteristic of false dreams and visions is emptiness or fruitlessness: *"For there shall no more be **any false, empty and fruitless vision** or flattering divination in the house of Israel"* (Ezek. 12:24).

Also, false dreams and visions leave the person with no hope and the message will not be confirmed by God: *"They have seen falsehood and lying divination, saying,*

'The Lord says,' but the Lord has not sent them. Yet they have hoped and made men to hope for confirmation of their word" (Ezek. 13:6 AMP).

The Lord Himself is against those who give false dreams and visions: *"Therefore thus says the Lord God, because you have spoken empty, false and delusive words and have seen lies, therefore behold, I am against you, says the Lord God. My hand shall be against the prophets who see empty, false and delusive visions and who give lying prophecies..."* (Ezek. 13:8-9 AMP).

Those who persist in giving false dreams and false visions, the Lord will not allow them into the secret council. *"They shall not be in the secret council of My people, nor shall they be recorded in the register of the house of Israel, nor shall they enter into the land, the land of Israel; and you shall know, (understand and realize) that I am the Lord God"* (Ezek. 13:9b AMP).

DISCERNING EVIL AND NATURAL INFLUENCES

I'd like to share how I discern evil and natural influences in my dreams. Ungodly influences occur even in true dreams and visions (those sent by God) and it is important to be able to recognize and handle them appropriately. This occurs in much the same way as satan was in God's special Garden—Garden of Eden—and the unguided response of Eve and subsequently Adam led to the fall of humankind from the original heightened level of spirituality and place in God.

The following is how you can discern evil influences or intrusions in your dream encounter.

- The presence of demonic influences or components can be reflected in the colors seen in that part or scene of the dream. When the color is predominantly black and white or mottled, the chances are high that a demonic presence is about. At such scenes, one should not take things on surface value only! Beware of deceptive appearances, phrases, or actions that may be present. Darkness often indicates the lack of God's light or a season of wilderness. This does not mean the entire dream is created by the devil, much the same as satan did not create the Garden of Eden, though his influence was dominant at the scene when he deceived Eve.

81

- Scenes of restricted liberty or movement in a dream or vision may indicate demonic presence or influences because as the Bible says, where the spirit of God is there is liberty. Restriction or inability to speak or move any part of the body in the dream indicates that the chance of demonic influence is very high. Also, the presence of undue fear or confusion should cause you to suspect the influence of the demonic.

- Scenes of accusations or condemnation resulting in low self-esteem or depression are not of God; Zechariah 3 illustrates this: *"Then he showed me Joshua the high priest standing before the angel of the Lord, and Satan standing at his right side to accuse him. The Lord said to Satan, 'The Lord rebukes you, Satan! The Lord, who has chosen Jerusalem, rebukes you! Is not this man a burning stick snatched from the fire?' Now Joshua was dressed in filthy clothes as he stood before the angel. The angel said to those who were standing before him, 'Take off his filthy clothes.' Then he said to Joshua, "See, I have taken away your sin, and I will put rich garments on you"* (Zech. 3:1-4).

Influences from the soul realm, the preoccupation of the dreamer, and the dreamer's mindset.

- Peter was hungry and God used his hunger to illustrate to Peter that Gentiles should be admitted into the Kingdom of God. Peter's mindset that salvation belongs only to Jews was dramatized and corrected (wrong mindset) using his hunger. Hunger is a desire of the flesh.

- Nebuchadnezzar wondered what would happen after his reign, and God revealed to him the empires that would come after his reign in Babylon (preoccupation of the dreamer). The dominant preoccupation of his mind at that time was the kingdom and rulership of Babylon.

- Joseph, the earthly father of Jesus, was contemplating how to divorce Mary when God told him to marry her (his thought life and preoccupation). This was therefore a direct answer to the questions arising from thoughts in his mind.

- God showed Jacob speckled and spotted ram in a dream in order to bring him to a place of economic prosperity (see Gen. 31:10-12). This dream was given to him within the background of his economic situation at his uncle's place: *"So Jacob sent word to Rachel and Leah to come out to the fields where his flocks were. He said to them, "I see that your father's attitude toward me is not what it was before, but the God of my father has been with me. You know that I've worked for your father with all my strength, yet your father has cheated me by changing my wages ten times. However, God has not allowed him to harm me"* (Gen. 31:4-7).

- God uses what we know to speak to us and to bring us from where we are to where He wants us to be in our earthly relationship with Him (the soul—mind, emotion, will—of the dreamer). This is also why we only dream in the language we speak and understand. Nobody receives dreams in a language that they do not understand. For instance, if you do not understand Russian language you will not receive a dream using Russian language.

- Paul's extreme Judaism and hatred toward Christians was corrected in a vision (mindset and preoccupation).

- King Abimelech's honest mistake was revealed to him and corrected in a dream (the mind) (see Gen. 20).

- Characters in a frequently watched soap opera will show up in the person's dreams because God will use what we know to explain what is yet to come (preoccupation and thought life).

In conclusion, soul influences in our dreams are important because they show us where we are wrong and keep us from the sword of God's destructive judgment: *"Why do you contend against Him? For He does not give account of any of His actions. [Sufficient for us it should be to know that it is He Who does them.] For God [does reveal His will; He] speaks not only once, but more than once, even though men do not regard it [including you, Job]. [One may hear God's voice] in a dream, in a vision of the night, when deep sleep falls on men while slumbering upon the bed, Then He opens the ears of men and seals their instruction [terrifying them with warnings], That He may withdraw man from his purpose and cut off pride from him [disgusting him with his own disappointing self-sufficiency]. He holds him back from the pit [of destruction], and his life from perishing by the sword [of God's destructive judgments]"* (Job 33:13-18 AMP).

Influences from bodily desires in dreams.

- Apostle Peter's hunger (his body's desire for food) was used in the ground-breaking vision that salvation belongs to the Jews and Gentiles: *"About noon the following day as they were on their journey and approaching the city, Peter went up on the roof to pray. He became hungry and wanted something to eat, and while the meal was being prepared, he fell into a trance. He saw heaven opened and something like a large sheet being let down to earth by its four corners. It contained all kinds of four-footed animals, as well as reptiles of the earth and birds of the air. Then a voice told him, Get up, Peter. Kill and eat. Surely not, Lord! Peter replied. I have never eaten anything impure or unclean. The voice spoke to him a second time, "Do not call anything impure that God has made clean. This happened three times, and immediately the sheet was taken back to heaven"* (Acts 10:9-16).

- Thirst can be used to dramatize a divine message, but always the essence of the spiritual connotation of the action remains.

- Persistent natural urge for sex can find expression in our dreams but that does not negate the deeper spiritual relevance. Sex in dreams is commoner in adolescents or young adults. What you spend time on you make room for. Persistent sexual encounters in dreams often indicate sexual lusts that have not been dealt with.

- The play-up of our flesh in dreams should help us to curb our excesses, for examples, excessive anger or fear.

Unfolding Understanding

Understanding of dreams occurs at different levels and often this differentiates the mature from the immature. A mature person or experienced dreamer will wait until proper understanding is gained before taking the required action.

- Understanding at the spirit level. Most often a dreamer has understanding in his spirit, though it may not yet be fruitful at his mind level or consciousness. Therefore for most parts, understanding at the spirit level is concealed or covert but potent until God gives the interpretation to the mind for human comprehension. Potent because though yet unrevealed to the mind, it propels and guides the dreamer to find the meaning of the dream at the mind level, and when he finds the correct meaning it resonates with his spirit and illuminates his mind.

- Understanding at the mind level. The human mind contains human memory, and it is here remembrance takes place. When the mind gets the correct understanding, the covert meaning already in the spirit confirms that the interpretation is correct.

- Understanding at the spirit level and at the mind level can occur at different times.

- You can have a revelation in your spirit and until you have attained a commensurate level of faith that the revelation demands, that revelation remains dormant and not released to your understanding in the mind.

- In this way, sometimes if the required level of faith comes much later from when the revelation was first received, the person may not be able to identify how the revelation was actually received.

- Once the revelation is released to the mind, the mind processes it.

- Processing involves understanding it in the common natural terms of the dreamer's mind and then applying it to the dreamer life situation. Application is correlating the revealed truth to relevance in the prevailing circumstance of the person.

- Proper application of the revealed truth is influenced by the peace and godly liberty the person enjoys.

- Hence whether you are a dreamer or an interpreter, the presence of the Holy Spirit in your life determines the level of understanding of your revelation and its eventual application.

The Holy Spirit Nudge

The Holy Spirit nudges me when I hear an incorrect interpretation of a dream. The following are examples of how the Holy Spirit may make people aware that something is not right.

- Feeling of uneasiness. For instance, Jacob pondered on the meaning of Joseph's dreams; even though he attempted some interpretation of the dream, he knew something was not sitting right within him.

- When the interpretation does not resonate with the dreamer; the interpretation bears no inner witness.

- Prompting a lack of concordance between the stated interpretation and the biblically acknowledged meaning of symbols and actions in the dream.

- Prompting a lack of smooth flow in the dream interpretation narratives; incoherent storyline in the interpretation.

- When more than two symbols do not agree with the purported storyline.

- When there are multiple focuses in the dream's interpretation; dreams always have one meaning and often one dominant essence but may have multiple applications.

- Prompting interpretation that is conflicting or contradicting scriptural principles or when the interpretation does not align with the Word of God.

- If it creates divisive tendency in a group.

- If the interpretation does not respect the life of other people even the life of a perceived enemy.

- If the interpretation does not speak of the love of God, no matter what.

- Interpretation must not exalt man; man is never above God.

- When the interpretation encourages the dreamer to take up vengeance (vengeance belongs to God).

- When interpretation encourages dependence on the interpreter.

CORPORATE APPROACH TO INTERPRETATION

My recipe for a corporate approach to interpreting dreams follows. Interpretation should:

- Fall along the lines of scriptural principles.
- Be confirmed before it is acted upon.
- Point people to Jesus, not lead them away from Him.
- Produce fruit of the Spirit, even if it is a warning.
- Seek to build up the church, even if it speaks of spiritual warfare.
- Submit to the ecclesiastical guidance.

Response to interpretation should not spiritualize everything; however, one should not fail to act on the prompting of the Holy Spirit for fear of over-spiritualizing things. Natural events may take up spiritual significance only if prompted by the Holy Spirit. Therefore, we must wait for rhema from God, before spiritualizing an event.

When interpreting for others, give short, concise, and precise interpretation to allow the person the opportunity to grasp the essence of the revelation.

The only reason God gives interpretation is to benefit the recipient and through the recipient benefit others. *"As for me, this mystery has been revealed to me, not because I have greater wisdom than other living men, **but so that you, O king,** may know the interpretation and that you may understand what went through your mind"* (Dan. 2:30).

Do not compel people to receive your interpretation. If they do not bear witness in their spirit to your interpretation, your interpretation may not be correct. Correct interpretation has the potential to break mindsets and negative strongholds. However, some dreamers may fail to acknowledge true interpretation because they are in a state of denial, even though inner witness exists. This is usually short-lived, as conviction by the Holy Spirit will eventually prevail.

All divine revelations come from God. The devil counterfeits this by sending information. The fact that you were not aware of something does not make it a revelation. Revelation is fresh illumination from Heaven.

In my experience, there are a few things you should *not* do:

- Do not rely on or become dependent on rigid symbol interpretation, or even on common sense. Rather, rely on the Holy Spirit. Ask the Lord for wisdom and understanding. Although interpreting dreams takes no great cleverness or special knowledge, it often takes years to develop a familiarity and sense of intimacy with the Lord to develop this lost art.

- Do not hesitate to get godly counsel from leaders and from those who have a history of understanding dreams.

- Do not fail to seek the Lord for the time application of a dream.

- Do not seek to control people with your dreams or through dream revelation. This may lead to manipulation. For instance, if you have a dream about someone you know, the Lord may be indicating that the person needs your prayers or the Lord may be speaking about you! Such revelation may be simply for your intercession and not meant to be shared with the person. Also, God may be revealing that you have similar traits as the person, which you are not aware of.

Other key points worthy of note:

1. Interpretation should not stir up dissension in any group.

2. Interpretation should not arm one section against another.

3. Interpretation should not rejoice at the punishment or fall of any person whether a perceived enemy or friend.

4. Ultimately, interpretation should lead to greater unity and closeness to God.

5. Interpretation may stir up actions and the need to address or confront issues so that peace will ensue.

6. Even if the interpretation brings rebuke, it should be given within a framework of godly assurance. God always keeps hope alive.

7. Good interpretation takes faith to a higher level.

Every one of us can receive true interpretation, but only if we seek the Lord, and always by the help of the Holy Spirit. The next chapter delves more deeply into the gift of interpretation.

ENDNOTE

1. Paula Price, *The Prophet's Dictionary* (New Kensington, PA: Whitaker House, 2006), 532.

POINTS TO PONDER

1. Handling warning dreams in fear may hasten the chance of the warning actually coming to pass in real life. Once you are fearful, your prayers are without faith and therefore ineffective. Have you experienced this situation?

2. The Bible speaks of dreams in two categories: those sent by God (true dreams or spiritual dreams) and false dreams not sent by God. Knowledge and wisdom of psychology is limited to dreams occurring only at the mind level that fall into the category that the Bible refers to as false dreams. Without this appreciation, many may find it hard to understand how biblical perspectives of dreams and visions differ from the knowledge of dreams in medical science. Do you understand the difference?

3. Because true dreams are imparted to your spirit, when you strengthen your spirit, dream experience will also be enhanced. The functional components of human spirit are: The wisdom of God (the life application of the Word of God). The conscience, (the laying aside of personal agenda). Communion (the art of spending intimate and quality time with God). Are you regularly strengthening your spirit?

Chapter 6

THE GIFT OF DREAM INTERPRETATION

I BELIEVE THAT THE GIFT of interpretation could be regarded as an off-shoot of the spirit of wisdom. Its manifestation is enhanced by the operation of the word of wisdom, the word of knowledge, and prophetic forth telling. Different authors have described the gift of interpretation in several ways.

In the book *The Prophet's Dictionary*, Paula Price gives the following definition of dream interpretation: *"Dream interpretation is the process whereby a prophet or prophetic vessel identifies a normal dream from one with distinct prophetic qualities. The prophet then applies prophetic insight, scriptural revelation, and symbol decipher-ing to uncover the message the Lord is sending into the world or into the life of the dreamer and his or her associates."[1]*

The Bible also records that it is rare to find a gifted interpreter of dreams.

> *For God speaketh once, yea twice, yet man perceiveth it not. In a dream, in a vision of the night, when deep sleep falleth upon men, in slumberings upon the bed; Then He openeth the ears of man, and sealeth their instruction. That He may withdraw man from his pur-pose and hide pride from man. He keepeth back his soul from the pit, and his life from perishing by the sword [destructive judgment]. He chastened also with pain upon his bed, with multitude of his bones with strong pains so that his life abhorreth bread, and his soul dainty*

*meat. His flesh is consumed away, that it cannot be seen and his bones that were not seen stick out. Yea, his soul draweth with unto the grave, and his life to the destroyers If there be a messenger with him, **an interpreter, one among a thousand** to show unto man his upright-ness* (Job 33:14-23 KJV).

The Amplified rendition of the verse is illuminating, *"[God's voice may be heard], **if there is for the hearer a messenger or an angel, an interpreter, one among a thousand to show** to man what is right for him, [how to be upright and in the right standing with God]"* (Job 33:23 AMP).

SOME KEY ATTRIBUTES OF THE GIFTED INTERPRETER

1. Pharaoh mentioned some key attributes of Joseph, a gifted dream inter-preter: *"And Pharaoh said to Joseph, 'I have had a dream, and there is no one who can interpret it. But I have heard it said of you that you **can understand a dream**, to **interpret it**.' So Joseph answered Pharaoh, say-ing, '**It is not me; God will give Pharaoh** an **answer of peace**'"* (Gen. 41:15-16).

   • Joseph understands the dream before interpreting it.

   • Joseph said it was not him but God who gives interpretation.

   • Joseph trusted that God would give Pharaoh the answer.

   • The answer will be an answer of peace even if it is a warning.

2. The Book of Daniel gives further key attributes of a gifted interpreter of dreams: *"Daniel answered in the presence of the king, and said, 'The secret which the king has demanded, the wise men, the astrologers, the magicians, and the soothsayers cannot declare to the king. But there a God in heaven who reveal secrets, and He has made known to King Nebucha-dnezzar what will be in latter days. Your dream, and the visions of your head upon your bed, were these: As for you, O King, thought came into your mind while on your bed, about what would come to pass after this; and He who reveals secrets has made known to you what will be. But as me, this secret has not been revealed to me because I have more wisdom*

than anyone living, but for our sakes who make known the interpretation to the King and that you may know the thoughts of your heart" (Dan. 2:27-30).

- Daniel believed that the wise men, the astrologers, the magicians, and the soothsayers could not declare interpretation.
- Only God can reveal the secret.
- God made it known because of the king.
- The interpreter does not know the interpretation because of his wisdom.

There are many *angelic interpreters* in the Bible but we see this gift in operation only in the lives of Joseph (of coat of many colors) and the prophet Daniel. By inference, we can deduce that the Bible says these messengers or interpreters should do the following: *"But if a messenger from heaven is there to intercede for him as a friend, to show him what is right, then God pities him and says 'Set him free. Do not make him die, for I have found a substitute. Then his body will become as healthy as a child's form and youthful again'"* (Job 33:23-25 TLB).

3. Notice from this passage, certain attributes that are expected of an interpreter. The interpreter should not only bring the essence of the dream message but also do the following:

- Intercede for the dreamer; "is there to intercede for him."
- Works from the heart of God with love and kindness; "as a friend." As we see in Daniel 4:19.
- Show the dreamer "what is right"; the word of wisdom or advice following the interpretation on the way forward. Daniel advised Nebuchadnezzar, *"Therefore, O king be pleased to accept my advice: Remember your sins by doing what is right, and your wickedness by being kind to the oppressed. It may be that then your prosperity will continue"* (Dan. 4:27).
- Help the dreamer to seek forgiveness from the Lord; "then God pities him and says Set him free. Do not make him die."
- Proclaim the redeeming blood of Jesus Christ, so that the dreamer will be restored again as in days of his youth; "I have found a

substitute. Then his body will become as healthy as a child's form and youthful again."

GIFTED INTERPRETERS IN THE BIBLE

In Joseph, the gift of interpretation was clearly evident in the later part of his life as well as when he was young. Later in life, *"Then the chief cupbearer said to Pharaoh, 'Today I am reminded of my shortcomings. Pharaoh was once angry with his servants, and he imprisoned me and the chief baker in the house of the captain of the guard. Each of us had a dream the same night, and each dream had a meaning of its own. Now a young Hebrew was there with us, a servant of the captain of the guard. We told him our dreams, and he interpreted them for us, giving each man the interpretation of his dream.* **And things turned out exactly as he interpreted them to us:** *I was restored to my position, and the other man was hanged'"* (Gen. 41:9-13).

In Daniel's life you will see not only this gift in operation but also how determination and commitment to God aided his quick growth in the anointing of his giftedness. Daniel is the epitome of a gifted and seasoned interpreter of dreams. No wonder the Bible says, *"...Daniel could understand visions and dreams of all kinds"* (Dan. 1:17).

Daniel was also described as being adept in understanding mysteries, able to explain riddles, and solve difficult problems.

> *The queen, hearing the voices of the king and his nobles, came into the banquet hall. "O king, live for ever!" she said. "Don't be alarmed! Don't look so pale! There is a man in your kingdom who has the spirit of the holy gods in him. In the time of your father he was found to have insight and intelligence and wisdom like that of the gods. King Nebuchadnezzar your father—your father the king, I say—appointed him chief of the magicians, enchanters, astrologers and diviners. This man Daniel, whom the king called Belteshazzar, was found to have a keen mind and knowledge and understanding, and also the ability to interpret dreams, explain riddles and solve difficult problems. Call for Daniel, and he will tell you what the writing means"* (Daniel 5:10-12).

INTERPRETING YOUR OWN DREAMS VERSUS OTHERS'

Every dreamer should seek God for proper understanding of his or her dreams. Nobody should ask others to help with dream interpretation without first seeking God's guidance, because God's sovereign choice of symbolism is such that it carries deep personal meaning and relevance that only the dreamer and God can truly appreciate. Everyone is capable of getting some useful understanding of his or her dreams by prayers and supplication. A gifted interpreter of dreams can help the dreamer come to the place where this appreciation is easily achieved. Interpreting dreams for other people is probably only effective when the interpreter has prophetic anointing. I believe some people have said that it is quite unsafe to interpret dreams for others if you do not have prophetic anointing, unless you are humble enough to put it as a suggestion rather than an interpretation. A true interpretation is not a compilation of meaning of symbols, but an inspired insight into the dream message. Dreamers have many chances to attempt the interpretation of their own dreams but only one chance with other people's dreams.

I believe interpretation of dreams should not sound equivocal at all but firm, though it should come with all humility. Interpretation should be as precise, unambiguous, and unequivocal as Joseph and Daniel put their interpretations firmly. Their interpretations stood firm and sure even before their fulfillment.

This is how the prophet Daniel stated one of his unequivocal interpretations in the Bible:

> *This is the meaning of the vision of the rock cut out of a mountain, but not by human hands—a rock that broke the iron, the bronze, the clay, the silver and the gold to pieces. "The great God has shown the king what will take place in the future. The dream is true and the interpretation is trustworthy"* (Daniel 2:45).

And Joseph was equally firm and sure of his interpretation, *"I cannot do it," Joseph replied to Pharaoh, "but God will give Pharaoh the answer he desires"* (Gen. 41:16).

God's desire is that everyone should come to a place of reasonable and valuable understanding of personal dreams and should always be reliant on the guidance of the Holy Spirit. I have found that all the components of prophecy are operational in the gift of interpretation of dreams and visions. These components are:

- Word of knowledge.
- Word of wisdom.
- Forthtelling; speaking the intentions of God.
- Foretelling; predictive prophecy.

A good knowledge of all the above components is crucial for proper operation of the gift of the interpretation of dreams particularly in the art of interpreting for others. However, I would like to emphasize that understanding one's own dreams is available to every dreamer, with or without prophetic anointing. God is the ultimate revealer of mysteries.

> Daniel replied, "No wise man, enchanter, magician or diviner can explain to the king the mystery he has asked about, but there is a God in heaven who reveals mysteries. He has shown King Nebuchadnezzar what will happen in days to come. Your dream and the visions that passed through your mind as you lay on your bed are these (Daniel 2:27-28).

Gaining Proficiency in Interpreting Dreams

Over the years, I have noticed that only those people who remember dreams on a consistent basis can become proficient at skillfully interpreting dreams. The gift of interpretation can be regarded as an offshoot of a prophetic anointing and those individuals who receive dreams and remember them consistently have some prophetic gifting. This does not mean they walk in the office of a prophet. A dream's covert meaning actually exists in the dreamer's spirit, but it may be unfruitful to the dreamer's mind until the true interpretation is given. When correct interpretation comes, the dreamer will usually acknowledge trustworthiness of that interpretation by inner witness.

Interpretation is an art made sharper by practice. The more dreams one interprets, the more proficient one becomes. Richness of the Word of God in the life of a person is the birth rock of his proficiency in dream interpretation.

The Power of Proclamation and the Gift of Interpretation

Some gifted interpreters have the power of proclamation, which is the divine inspiration to declare an option out of more than one possibility. This power of proclamation becomes valuable when the dreamer wakes up prior to, or one is faced with endless possibilities, or awoke at a moment of decision in a dream. When this occurs, God is usually leaving room for the dreamer to intercede and help influence the situation's eventual outcome. A person with the power of proclamation can add his agreement in faith to help a dreamer and so may help tilt the balance in the desired direction.

FACTORS OPERATING IN THE GIFT OF INTERPRETATION

Though those with the gift of interpretation are rare, it is important that they are properly trained for equipping other saints of God. I have met some people who appear to be gifted in the interpretation of dreams, but unfortunately some of these gifted people only walk in the elementary stages of the anointing. Some of the factors that could help such people to move to a place of active operation in the gift of interpretation are:

1. A heart of love is a prerequisite.

Dream interpretation is much more than a compilation of dream symbols and actions. Behind every interpretation of a dream must be revelation of the eternal character of God. We should pursue the understanding of our dreams and visions and allow the ways of God to be so revealed in us as to place us in the position where we can totally trust God. In this way we can become more dependent on the incorruptible Word of God. It is also worthy to note that in interpreting dreams for others, interpretation must be given from the heart of God—a heart full of God's love—otherwise the interpreter runs the risk of giving views clouded with sentiment and emotion. Very importantly, we must know that no matter how gifted an interpreter is, his ability to interpret dreams is always proportional to the lordship of the Word of God over his life. God gives interpretation for the benefit of the dreamer (see Daniel 2:29-30).

2. The word of wisdom.

Spiritual Wisdom is sound judgment, sagacity, prudent learning, or erudition that comes from God. By wisdom you gain an understanding of what is true and right. Wisdom from God is a spirit that can be acquired, transferred, or given as a gift from the Holy Spirit.

On the other hand, the word of wisdom is wisdom divinely given for a particular situation and is an offshoot of spiritual wisdom.

> *There are different kinds of gifts, but the same Spirit. There are different kinds of service, but the same Lord. There are different kinds of working, but the same God works all of them in all men. Now to each one the manifestation of the Spirit is given for the common good. To one there is given through* **the Spirit the message** [**the word**] *of wisdom, to another* **the message** [**the word**] *of knowledge by means of the same Spirit, to another faith by the same Spirit, to another gifts of healing by that one Spirit, to another miraculous powers, to another prophecy, to another distinguishing between spirits, to another speaking in different kinds of tongues, and to still another the interpretation of tongues. All these are the work of one and the same Spirit, and He gives them to each one, just as He determines* (1 Corinthians 12:4-11).

Characteristically, a word of wisdom comes as a momentary gift from the Holy Spirit. It is not a resident gift in any person but sprouts from the resident spiritual wisdom in the person at the point of need.

Word of wisdom is the spirit of wisdom applied or made relevant for a given situation. It can come to the person in several ways, but is commonly manifested in the following manners:

- As instanteous divine knowledge or insight for a given circumstance.
- As divinely inspired wise utterance for life in the situation.
- As sharpness of mind to birth key solutions to a problem.

Let us look at some instances in the Bible when the operation of the word of wisdom is demonstrated:

For I will give you words and wisdom that none of your adversaries will be able to resist or contradict (Luke 21:15).

This man Daniel, whom the king called Belteshazzar, **was found to have a keen mind and knowledge and understanding, and also the ability to interpret dreams, explain riddles and solve difficult problems.** *Call for Daniel, and he will tell you what the writing means* (Daniel 5:12).

The Sovereign Lord has given me **an instructed tongue, to know** *the* **word that sustains the weary.** *He wakens me morning by morning, wakens my ear to listen like one being taught* (Isaiah 50:4).

It was through a word of wisdom that Solomon resolved the delicate situation that arose between two prostitutes. Solomon's unimaginable but bold proposal to the two prostitutes to divide the living child coerced the truth into the open and brought a quick end to an ugly situation. It is only within a flourishing spiritual wisdom that the operation of the word of wisdom can be manifested, *"God gave Solomon wisdom and very great insight, and a breadth of understanding as measureless as the sand on the seashore"* (1 Kings 4:29). It was in that context that the crucial word of wisdom for resolving that intricate situation came to King Solomon.

In practical terms, the operation of the word of wisdom helps the interpreter expound the relevance of the symbols and actions in the dream to the dreamer's personal life situation (see Dan. 2:36-45).

Here, the interpretation that the prophet Daniel gave was by word of wisdom, by which he correlated the superiority of gold and silver to the superiority of King Nebuchadnezzar over the subsequent empires that come after him. By word of wisdom he was also able to relate the inability of the iron and clay to mix to the lack of unity that would exist in the fourth empire.

3. The word of knowledge and the interpretation of dreams.

A word of knowledge is the spiritual gift of knowing information beyond natural means, as through God's revelation: *"To one there is given through the Spirit the message of wisdom, to another the message* [word] *of knowledge by means of the same Spirit"* (1 Cor. 12:8).

This is the process by which God gives clues to the essence of the dream to the dreamer. The clue would usually be beyond what the dreamer could logically figure out. Word of knowledge interpretation comes without necessarily expounding on the relevance of the symbols in the dream. Most people in an established prophetic ministry will get dream interpretation in this way. Quite often, it is not uncommon for some prophets to get the correct and true essence of the dream without actually knowing the exact relevance of the symbols in the dream. This is also how some believers think of Bible verses upon waking from a dream. God also uses this method to give hints of meaning of dreams to unbelievers.

Word of knowledge interpretation for every dream interpreter. Many prophetic people interpret dreams by a word of knowledge rather than through the gift of interpretation. Such people often cannot explain how they arrived at an interpretation on the basis of a dream's elements.

Word of knowledge interpretation, however, will usually not relate the relevance of a dream's elements to the life circumstances of the dreamer. So, in that sense, it is restricted in details. There's enough detail to keep the dreamer from falling into a disastrous mistake, but every word of knowledge interpretation should be complemented with an acquired skill of interpretation (more about that soon).

Word of knowledge interpretation reveals only a certain percentage of a dream's full meaning; therefore, it may be short on the keys of wisdom inherent in dreams. Nevertheless, word of knowledge interpretation always gives the correct essence of dream's message. Most angelic interpretations in the Bible appear to be word of knowledge interpretations. Yet, if asked, the angels gave further exposition on elements of the dreams or visions. Having a word of knowledge is the most common way that dreamers with undeveloped interpretative skills can gain understanding of dreams.

Divine Prompting

It is by the operation of the word of knowledge that the interpreter is prompted to what God might be specifying or highlighting in the dream. It is also by the word of knowledge that the Holy Spirit highlights a key action, phrase, image, or word in the dream. This helps in the understanding of the dream. Such prompting would otherwise be unavailable to the interpreter or the dreamer without the help of the Holy Spirit.

Not waiting to receive divine prompting is a principal cause for wrong interpretation. Divine prompting gives divine guidance for the use of human reasoning and thereby aids the interpretation of the dream.

Divine prompting in dream interpretation is characterized by the fact that:

- Every element in the dream should agree with the prompting.
- The context, trend, and background of the dream should also line up with the divine promoting.
- The divine prompting should be capable of guiding the eventual, logical exposition of the dream's symbols and actions.
- The dream message should hinge on this prompting.

This prompting comes as:

- Inner knowing.
- Birthing in your spirit.
- Illumination of an action or symbol or phrase or even a single word mentioned in the dream often very hard to put aside.
- Quickening to a Bible passage.

How long does it take to get a divine prompting? For me there is no special time frame within which the prompting can come for interpretation. It is a highly variable occurrence. It can take a long time to come or come spontaneously. However, with practice, divine prompting for an interpretation is facilitated to come quickly to a seasoned interpreter. Such as, it can come:

- If the dreamer waits on God and asks Him for prompting.
- Instantaneously, the dreamer doesn't have to wait days or weeks or months.
- Only after the dreamer has carefully prayed about it.

Key points in word of knowledge interpretation:

- God sows the meaning of the dream into the person's mind without necessarily expounding on the relevance of the dream symbols.

- Knowing something beyond natural means of the mind because it comes by God's revelation.

- Most interpretations given by angels in the Scriptures are word of knowledge interpretation.

- Needs to be complemented by acquired skills of interpretation to bring meaning to the dream and to gain wisdom keys inherent in the dream.

- The means by which God gives unbelievers hints of their dream's meaning.

- Commonly the way God gives Bible verses related to the meaning of the dream.

The following is a biblical example of a dream and its interpretation.

- The Dream

  Then the angel who talked with me returned and wakened me, as a man is wakened from his sleep. He asked me, "What do you see?" I answered, "I see a solid gold lampstand with a bowl at the top and seven lights on it, with seven channels to the lights. Also there are two olive trees by it, one on the right of the bowl and the other on its left." I asked the angel who talked with me, "What are these, my lord?" (Zechariah 4:1-4)

- The Interpretation

  He answered, "Do you not know what these are?" "No, my lord," I replied. So he said to me, "This is the word of the Lord to Zerubbabel: 'Not by might nor by power, but by My Spirit,' says the Lord Almighty" (Zechariah 4:5-6).

I believe this probably means that as long as Zerubbabel remains connected to the source of anointing—as symbolized by the two channels connecting the bowl and the two olive trees—then the light (the Spirit) will continue to burn in him. It will not be by might nor by power, but by the Spirit of the Almighty that Zerubbabel will succeed.

Word of knowledge operating in the gift of interpretation. We see the operation of the word of knowledge in Daniel and Joseph's interpretations.

By the word of knowledge, Daniel was prompted to know that the head of gold of the image of the great statue represented King Nebuchadnezzar's dream, *"in your hands he has placed mankind and the beasts of the field and the birds of the air. Wherever they live, he has made you ruler over them all.* **You are that head of gold** (Dan. 2:38).

Without this prompting, Daniel would not have been able to know this or put the story together with the message of the dream. After obtaining this prompting, Daniel was then able to apply minimal logical deduction on the whole of the dream symbols and actions. We see in another instance when Daniel could not get away from a prompting of a dream, which came to him in the form of "the boastful horn."

> *Then I wanted to know the true meaning of the fourth beast, which was different from all the others and most terrifying, with its iron teeth and bronze claws—the beast that crushed and devoured its victims and trampled underfoot whatever was left. I also wanted to know about the ten horns on its head and about the other horn that came up, before which three of them fell—the horn that looked more imposing than the others and that had eyes and a mouth that spoke boastfully* (Daniel 7:19-20).

Joseph was divinely prompted by the word of knowledge to the meaning of the seven cows.

> *Then Joseph said to Pharaoh, "The dreams of Pharaoh are one and the same. God has revealed to Pharaoh what he is about to do.* **The seven good cows are seven years, and the seven good ears of corn are seven years; it is one and the same dream.** *The seven lean, ugly cows that came up afterward are seven years, and so are the seven worthless*

ears of corn scorched by the east wind: They are seven years of famine (Genesis 41:25-27).

By this divine prompting, the operation of the word of knowledge, Joseph was able to know that the seven cows and ears of corn represent seven years. With this prompting, the interpretation was set in order; and without this prompting, Joseph would not have received the correct interpretation.

4. Prophetic forthtelling.

In general, the term *prophetic forthtelling* means speaking the mind or intentions of God. Likewise, a true and correct interpretation of a dream should reveal the mind of God in sending the dream. Therefore, forthtelling is an essential component of the operation of the gift of interpretation of dreams. The Psalmist made the point very clear when describing Joseph's interpretation as prophetic: *"They bruised his feet with shackles, his neck was put in iron till what **he foretold came to pass,** till the word of the Lord proved him true,"* (Ps. 105:18-19). In this instance. Joseph gave the mind of God regarding the dreams that he interpreted that were later fulfilled in the lives of the dreamers.

Prophetic forthtelling helps the interpreter put together the word of wisdom and the word of knowledge in the dream to bring out the message in the dream. The message of a dream is the true essence of the dream or the true reason behind the dream. It is not enough to compile a list of the meanings of the various dream symbols but rather to truly and correctly interpret, one has to able to answer the question: why was the dream sent? It is the operation of the prophetic forthtelling that helps the interpreter answer this key question.

Prophetic forthtelling:

- Flows from the heart of love because God is love, and if it is said in love, the pronouncements will come out with divine power.

- May not immediately appear to be a prophetic utterance, often sounds as wise saying from a person in a trusted godly position. In Deuteronomy 17:14-20 (see following), we see Moses' prophetic forthtelling.

- Prophetic forthtelling should contain divine insight for present and future positions.

The interpreter's ability to correctly proclaim the essence of the dream message (function of prophetic forthtelling) is enhanced by:

- Having the mind of Christ, having a yielded personal will, having the peace of God that surpasses all understanding, and operating in the unconditional love of God.
- Being led always by the Holy Spirit, "as many as are led by the Spirit of God, they are the sons of God."
- Breaking the bonds of wickedness or the work of outer man in a dreamer's life, so the spirit man can be expressed unhindered.
- Leading a life of persistent prayer.
- Living a life of sacrifice and paying due attention to intercession for other people.

All correct interpretation comes by the help of the Holy Spirit, although the actual way He does this varies. The Holy Spirit works either through a word of knowledge, a gift of interpretation, or a process of acquired interpretative skills.

God also gives dreams to unbelievers, and when He wishes to give them some understanding, He sows the dream's essence into the unbeliever's mind. This sowing may come as an impression, a flash of idea, or a knowing in the dreamer's mind. In this way, Pilate's wife had some understanding of her dream, and the Magi understood not to return via their arrival route because of Herod's evil intentions.

5. Acquired skills.

Acquired skills is the process by which you understand dreams through the meaning of symbols or how symbols were used in previous dream encounters, or by use of a personal dictionary of dreams symbols. With acquired skills of interpretation, a dreamer may apply a correctly derived "personal dictionary" of dream symbols in the interpretative process.

Every dreamer needs these skills in addition to any giftedness. Interpretation is a studied art made sharper by practice, but few Christians consider acquiring this wonderful skill to be worthwhile. Yet it's a great resource in gaining some understanding of dreams. Whether you are gifted in interpretation or not, all need to be able to properly expound on the relevance of symbols in a dreamer's life.

Key *points* in acquired skills of interpretation of dreams:

- Proficient interpretation of dreams is not only a gift but a reward of diligent study and seeking the Lord.

- Acquiring skills means gaining understanding of your dreams by applying a correctly derived personal dream vocabulary.

- Acquired skills is the means by which the Holy Spirit prompts the dreamer to the relevance of the dream symbols to the dreamer's personal circumstance.

- A means by which exposition is given to the symbol relevance to the dreamer circumstance and unfolds the hidden ways or strategy for fulfilling the goals of the dream or vision.

Key *actions* in acquired skills of interpretation:

- Waiting for the prompting of the Holy Spirit before applying the personal vocabulary of dream symbols.

- Understanding the meaning of the symbols and symbolic actions.

- Prayerfully determining the story line or plot of the dream message; this is what God might be saying to the dreamer in the dream.

- Properly expounding the relevance of each symbol to the dreamer's life circumstance; this will bring out the wisdom keys for the fulfillment of the dream message.

ENDNOTE

1. Paula Price, *The Prophet's Dictionary* (New Kensington, PA: Whitaker, 2006), 418.

POINTS TO PONDER

1. The gift of interpretation could be regarded as an offshoot of the spirit of wisdom. Its manifestation is enhanced by the operation of the word of wisdom, the word of knowledge, and prophetic forthtelling. How well do you understand these concepts?

   _____

   _____

2. You should seek God for proper understanding of your dreams. You should not ask others to help with dream interpretation without first seeking God's guidance, because God's sovereign choice of symbolism is such that it carries deep personal meaning and relevance that only you the dreamer and God can truly appreciate. Do you seek God's guidance first?

   _____

   _____

3. Every dreamer needs interpretations skills in addition to any gifted-ness. Interpretation is a studied art made sharper by practice, but few Christians consider acquiring this wonderful skill to be worthwhile. Do you?

   _____

   _____

Chapter 7

SCRIPTURAL EXAMPLES OF DREAMS AND VISIONS

STUDYING EXAMPLES OF how dreams were interpreted in the Bible is not only instructive but also thoroughly interesting and helpful in the understanding of the mysteries of God. It is as though special anointing lifts off the pages of the Bible to the reader. Such impartation sharpens and seasons the reader's mind and sets the stage for future godly interpretation.

The following Bible interpretations are classic examples for how to correctly interpret dreams, and they allow us to learn to interpret and draw godly conclusions from our own dreams. It is my hope as you study some of them in this chapter that your confidence will be built up ready to make meaning out of the dreams you receive. Remember that Daniel had understanding of all kinds of dreams and visions (see Dan. 1:17), so likewise it is quite possible to gain some understanding of a good proportion or all of *your* dreams.

The scriptural examples given in this chapter are of those dreams whose interpretations are generally agreed on or accepted, or are dreams fulfilled by subsequent events in the Scripture, or those whose interpretations were actually given by God Himself.

NEBUCHADNEZZAR'S DREAM OF THE LARGE STATUE (DANIEL 2:31-41).

Dream	Meaning	Points to Note
An enormous, dazzling statue awesome in appearance. The head of the statue was made of pure gold, its chest and arms of silver, its belly and thighs of bronze, its legs of iron, its feet part iron and part baked clay.	Worshiping of statues was prevalent in Nebuchadnezzar's time hence it played up in his dream. Later in his life he attempted to create this great statue as an idol for worshiping (Daniel 3).	*Babylon* would be the first world power according to this dream. Notice the dreamer was not *directly participating* in this dream, *yet the dream was about him* and his kingdom; so absolute reliance on the Holy Spirit rather than facts and figures or set of rules.
A rock was cut out, but not by human hands.	*Divine and sovereign intervention.*	Sometimes in dream situations, the dreamer may see, perceive or know things while in the dream that usually go beyond the realm of the capacity of the natural sense. *"A rock cut not with human hands"* connotes knowledge beyond the immediate awareness or environment.
The wind swept them away without leaving a trace.	*All the kingdoms will eventually be wiped away by the Kingdom of God and Jesus Christ.*	The wind here is the symbol of the move of God or the Spirit of God.
But the rock that struck the statue became a huge mountain and filled the whole earth.	*The Kingdom of God shall cover the whole earth.*	The kingdom of this world will eventually disappear and in its place the Kingdom of God shall stand forever.

Dream	Meaning	Points to Note
You, O king, are the king of kings.	*Nebuchadnezzar and his kingdom comprise the head of gold. A head of fine gold is the symbol of Babylon and King Nebuchadnezzar.*	*The head of the statue made of gold refers to the Babylonian empire personified by Nebuchadnezzar.* This is the operation of the word of knowledge and of the word of wisdom in the giftedness of Daniel, the interpreter.
"After you, another kingdom will rise, inferior to yours."	*Silver is considered inferior to gold.* **The chest and arms** *of silver represent the* **Medo-Persia** *empire.*	*Medo-Persia* would become the second world power after defeating Babylon. Applying minimal logical deduction, the second kingdom, represented by silver shall be inferior to that represented by gold. The mind and intellect should only come into interpretation of dreams after the Holy Spirit has prompted the dreamer or the interpreter.
Next, a third kingdom, one of bronze, will rule over the whole earth.	*As bronze is considered inferior to silver.* **The belly and thighs** *of bronze represent* **Greece.**	*Greece* would emerge as the third world power after defeating the Medo-Persia empire. Another application of minimal logical deduction. Greece will be inferior to Medo-Persia, even as bronze is considered inferior to silver.

Dream	Meaning	Points to Note
Finally, there will be a fourth kingdom, strong as iron—for iron breaks and smashes everything.	*Iron is inferior to bronze, but iron is generally known for being strong, so although inferior to bronze, this kingdom will have the strength to conquer other kingdoms.* *The **leg of iron and the feet of iron and clay** symbolized the **Roman empire**.*	*Rome* would defeat Greece and become the fourth world power. The strength of this kingdom is played out in this dream dramatization with the symbol of iron. The focus is shifted from *value* of the metal to comparative *strength*. *Leg* is symbolic of what you stand on; iron represents strength, this kingdom will focus on shear strength. *The fourth kingdom,* generally identified as *Rome*, became divided into two as represented by the *two legs*—the eastern and western empires. Later still these two were divided into *ten* that formed the confederacy of European nations; just as the two legs of the large statue end in ten toes. This is the level of accuracy and precision that dream interpretation should attain in the end time.

Dream	Meaning	Points to Note
Just as the feet and toes were part baked clay and part iron, so this will be a divided kingdom; yet it will have some of the strength of iron, even as iron is mixed with clay.	*The mixture of iron and clay indicate that this kingdom, despite its strength, will lack coherent unity. It will be a divided kingdom.*	The weakness of the fourth strong kingdom is that it lacked unity. *Feet* often symbolize attitudes of the heart. *Clay* is the symbol for frailty or weakness of humanity. Put together means that this kingdom, though strong, will suffer from lack of unity just as clay and iron cannot mix mainly due to poor attitude of hearts (symbolized by feet) of the emerged leaders.
Daniel 2:34-35 *While you were watching, a rock was cut out, but not by human hands. It struck the statue on its feet of iron and clay and smashed them.*		In the dream, the gold, silver, and bronze were crushed at the same time as the legs of iron and the feet of clay and iron, obscuring the actual sequence of the rise and fall of the successive kingdoms. Therefore in dream interpretation, one should continuously rely on the Holy Spirit for the godly insight embedded in divine symbolism, as the sequence of events and the limitation in time could be obscured in the dream's dramatization. Events that may span or transcend decades in actual occurrence, may be portrayed in a few minutes in the dream's drama.

DANIEL'S DREAM OF FOUR BEASTS (DANIEL 7).

(Notice the correlation of this dream with Nebuchadnezzar of the large statue; the same essence or storyline but remarkably different symbolism according to what the dreamer is accustomed to.)

Dream	Meaning	Points to Note
Four winds of heaven churning up the great sea.	*The events as orchestrated from the heaven.*	The great sea represents the restless humanity, the nations of the world. The winds of heaven indicate the move of God that would bring change in the seasons. The Bible says, *"He changes the times and the seasons";* reflection of the social and political agitations in the kingdoms of the world.
Four great beasts, each different from the other.	*The beasts symbolize power that will rule the land, each different from the other.*	The different beasts signify the power of successive empires as characterized by a specific type of force associated with the animal.
Came up out of the sea.	*The product or work of humanity.*	Sea is often the symbol of humanity, nations, or masses of people.
The first was like a lion with wings of an eagle.	*Babylon*	A *lion* symbolizes the strength of Babylon, the king of beasts. An *eagle* represents the swiftness, the prophetic anointing of the king. The eagle is the king of the birds. The *wings* that were torn off indicate the humiliation that the king will suffer.

Dream	Meaning	Points to Note
The second beast looked like a bear with three ribs in its mouth.	*Medo-Persia Empire*	A bear goes for what belongs to others by force.
The beast that devoured flesh.	*Medo-Persia Empire*	Devoured Babylon.
The three ribs.	*The kingdoms of Babylon, Libya and Egypt.*	The *three empires* that were conquered by the bear—Medo-Persia.
The leopard with four wings and four heads.	**Greece** **Four wings** *symbolize the universality and speed with which the empire will operate.* **Four heads** *represent the four governments that would arise after the death of Alexander the Great.*	The *leopard* is known as the most agile and gracious; with great rapidity it conquered the whole world. This kingdom will be like the leopard as it conquered the nations. Generally believed to be Greece under the leader of Alexander the Great.
The four heads.	*Stands for Egypt, Syria, Thrace, and Macedonia*	*After Alexander's death,* his empire was divided among his four army generals.

Dream	Meaning	Points to Note
The great beast with iron teeth and ten horns.	**Roman Empire** *Daniel 7:23—"the fourth beast is a fourth kingdom that will appear on Earth. It will be different from all the other kingdoms and will devour the whole Earth, trampling it down and crushing it."*	The beast did not fit into any known description of animal, but it was dreadful, terrifying, and strong. The *horn* represents power and authority. The *little horn* began small but became the greatest.
The boastful little horn.	*anti-Christ*	Arrogance and the presumption of the *anti-Christ*.
"As I looked, thrones were set in place, and the Ancient of Days took His seat. A river of fire was flowing, coming out from before Him. …The court was seated, and the books were opened.	**The judgment of God** *was approaching; God will judge all seen and unseen.* **Court** indicates **trial is imminent** *or that the* **time of trial** *has already come.*	The Word of God will both teach and reproach us if we allow it. *Ancient of days* refers to God the Father. *River of fire* refers to impending judgment. This is an example of a heavenly court session when God presides as the Judge over a spiritual court-like scenario. Dreams of heavenly court scenes are common.

SCRIPTURAL EXAMPLES OF DREAMS AND VISIONS

Dream	Meaning	Points to Note
But the court will sit, and his power will be taken away and completely destroyed forever. Then the sovereignty, power and greatness of the kingdoms under the whole heaven will be handed over to the saints, the people of the Most High. His Kingdom will be an everlasting Kingdom, and all rulers will worship and obey Him.	*The kingdom of this world will become the Kingdom of God and His Christ.*	The redeemed of the Lord (the saints of God) will *triumph and rule with the Lord.*
Angelic interpretation. Daniel 7:15-18—"I, Daniel, was troubled in spirit, and the visions that passed through my mind disturbed me. I approached one of those standing there and asked him the true meaning of all this."	*Angelic interpretations are often brief and give an overview (see also Zechariah 4:1-6).*	This is akin to a word of *knowledge type of interpretation.* In most places in the Bible, angel interpreters give a word of knowledge type of interpretation in which they only give a short panoramic view of the meaning or essence of the dream. A word of knowledge is the means by which one supernaturally knows what is beyond the natural mind to know.

Dream	Meaning	Points to Note
Daniel had further prompting that lingered on. Daniel 7:19-20— "Then I wanted to know the true meaning of the fourth beast, which was different from all the others…the horn that looked more imposing than the others and that had eyes and a mouth that spoke boastfully."	*Further exposition given by the angel interpreter* *(see Daniel 7:24-27).*	Angelic interpretation will give *detailed exposition and show the relevance of the symbolic overtone/ implication when asked.*

NEBUCHADNEZZAR'S DREAM OF THE ENORMOUS TREE (DANIEL 4:10-37).

Dream	Meaning	Points to Note
An enormous tree in the middle of the land grew large and strong; its top reached the sky visible to the ends of the earth.	*You, O king are the tree! You have become great and strong—reaching the sky.* *Symbolically, a tree could stand for leader or ruler.* ***Birds and beasts** could represent leaders, or kingdoms or nations; evil or good.* *Birds and beasts in dreams could also be symbolic of spirits. For example, a **dove** is symbolic of the Holy Spirit; a **vulture**, evil spirit or an opportunist.*	In biblical times, the people were primarily agriculturists and illustrated human greatness and power by the figure of a **grown tree**. **Birds and beasts** gathering under the tree was symbolic of the **varied people groups** under the sceptre of Nebuchadnezzar's authority.
A messenger, a Holy One coming down from Heaven.	The decree of the Most High issued down from Heaven from God. God sometimes speaks into our dreams and may use notable spiritual leaders or angels to bring timely messages to us.	One of the reasons *God speaks* into our dreams and visions is to establish His decision or His truth as in this proclamation of punishment for the king's pride.

Dream	Meaning	Points to Note
Cut down the tree, trim off its branches, scatter its fruit.	*The kingdom will be taken from Nebuchadnezzar.*	The judgment on Nebuchadnezzar. Symbolic of the *humiliation the king would suffer.*
But let the stump and his root bound with iron and bronze remain in the ground in the grass of the field. Let his mind be changed from that of man to that of animal.	*Because its root remains, the kingdom will be restored to the king when he acknowledges God. Binding by chains of iron and bronze means captivity, insanity.* **Root** *stands for that which keeps something alive, keeps hope alive, or means of survival or restoration.* **The chains of iron =** *bondage.*	*The root that remains* is symbolic of the fact that Nebuchadnezzar would be restored as he was restored after the humiliation. *The chains of iron* symbolize the bondage as indicated by the bondage that came upon his mind. Notice the superimposition: the figure of speech changed from that of a tree *"Let the stump"* to that of human being *"Let his mind be."* In this case, the superimposition indicates that the tree was symbolic of a man.
Let him be drenched with the dew of heaven and let him live among the animals and plants of the earth till seven times pass by him.	*Driven away from his people and lives with wild animals, will eat grass until seven times will pass by.*	Lived like an animal, like the beast of the earth for a period.

Dream	Meaning	Points to Note
Daniel 4:19 Then Daniel (also called Belteshazzar) was greatly perplexed for a time, and his thoughts terrified him. So the king said, "Belteshazzar, do not let the dream or its meaning alarm you." Belteshazzar answered, "My lord, if only the dream applied to your enemies and its meaning to your adversaries!"		The godly interpreter should have the compassion of God as demonstrated by Daniel's concern for the king. Love and compassion and readiness to see things from God's perspective are the divine security in avoiding presumptuous error and inadvertent judgment in interpreting dreams.
Daniel 4:27-28 "Therefore, O king, be pleased to accept my advice: Renounce your sins by doing what is right, and your wickedness by being kind to the oppressed. It may be that then your prosperity will continue." All this happened to King Nebuchadnezzar.		The prophet Daniel seems to confirm that dreams are only potential events and if we take the appropriate action, the danger warned about could be avoided. Unfortunately King Nebuchadnezzar failed to heed the advice given him and the calamity came upon him.

King Nebuchadnezzar's dream of the enormous tree is similar to the parable of Great Cedar described in Ezekiel 31:3-17.

God described Ezekiel as the watchman to the house of Israel and He used extensive symbolism in most of His communications. Let us see how we can understand the symbolism in Ezekiel's vision of the valley of dry bones. In his vision are multiple dimensions to symbolism.

The vision is written about in Ezekiel 37:1-10. The interpretation given by God is found in Ezekiel 37:11-14.

Symbol	Meaning	Inspired Interpretation
A collection of dry bones; littering a valley floor.	A state of hopelessness; extreme hardship; impossibility.	A situation that is humanly impossible.
Scattered.	Jews scattered throughout the nations.	
The bones (hopeless situation) came together and assembled into skeletons (bone to his bones).	Coming together as predestined, each bone identified the exact skeleton to which it originally belonged.	Coming together of the Jews to a state of their own as prophesied.
As he observed, flesh and skin grew on the skeleton.	This speaks of comfort and protection from God that will eventually emerge, particularly during the process.	The comfort and protection of God when we encounter trials in the process of obeying God.
The bodies stayed dead, until a dramatic moment when God put breath into them.	Not filled with the spirit of God until the time appointed for this to happen.	After the restoration and recovery from the dead situation, the people remained spiritually dead. Their old souls needed to be renewed. The word *breath* also means spirit, and the vision is reminiscent of Genesis 2:7 where God breathes life into the first man.

Symbol	Meaning	Inspired Interpretation
Come from the four winds.	The role of the four corners of the world in the eventual salvation of Israel.	God is saying that it would take a miracle to bring the remnants of Israel back together from many locations or nations where they are scattered. Israel will need an even greater miracle to be spiritually born-again with the Spirit of God.
Vast army.	The eventual strength of the army of Israel, as it shall be like the army of the Lord.	

VISIONS OF THE LIVING CREATURES AT THE THRONE ROOM OF GOD

The living creatures transport the throne of God. In Ezekiel chapters 1 and 10, the prophet Ezekiel saw the throne of God in motion being carried by the living creatures. They are also creatures of the highest level of revelations. See Ezekiel 10:13-17, Ezekiel 1:4-10, and Revelation 4:6-8.

The four aspects of the nature of God.

The four faces of these creatures as seen through the eyes of Ezekiel and apostle John portray aspects of the character of God. Their likeness to the form of earthly creatures being only representative of the aspects of God's character that is symbolized. The four faces symbolize God's rule over all creation.

Symbol Reflected by the Four Faces	Aspect of God Portrayed	Symbolic Connotations in Dreams and Visions
The face of a lion	*Majesty, power or strength, supremacy, and courage*	Power, strength, or majesty
The face of a ox	*Faithfulness, perseverance, patience, and servanthood*	Faithfulness, endurance, servanthood
The face of a man	*Intelligence, royalty (nobility), and wisdom, frailty*	Frailty, nobility, human wisdom
The face of an eagle	*Sovereignty or divinity, devotion, deity, and divine mystery*	Devotion, focus, the prophetic

Perhaps as some have suggested, the four faces of the living creatures, are symbolic of the four portraits of Jesus as given in the four Gospels:

- Matthew represents our Lord as the King—the Lion
- Mark portrays Him as the Servant—the Ox
- Luke emphasizes His humanity—Man
- John proclaims especially His deity—the Eagle

Factors to Remember

1. Place reliance on the Holy Spirit and acknowledgment that it is God who reveals the mystery.
   - Daniel 2:26-28
   - Genesis 41:16
2. God gives interpretation for the benefit of the dreamer.
   - Daniel 2:30
   - Genesis 41:28
3. Interpretation reflects meaning of dream elements/events/actions whose understanding is prompted by God. Understanding that could only have come from God.
   - Seven cows = seven years
   - Head of statue = King Nebuchadnezzar
4. Interpretation reflects overtone of the key elements or actions.
   - Change from gold to silver, change from superior to less superior
   - Ugly and lean = famine
   - Fat and sleek = prosperity
   - Together = unity
5. Interpretation contains pockets of prophetic unction.
   - Daniel 2:42-43
   - Genesis 41:26-32
6. Interpretation contains evidence of godly word of wisdom.
   - Genesis 41:33-37
   - Daniel 2 44-47

COURT-LIKE AUDIENCE WITH GOD IN DREAMS AND VISIONS

Court-like audience with God (a spiritual court session) in dreams and visions is any court-scenario visionary encounter in which God presides. In general, they are not uncommon experiences, though many people may not notice them. Judgments from these court audiences with God are fair and balanced perspectives of the situations and events because they emanate from God's presence and judgment. In these heavenly courts, everything is laid bare, as God is the Judge. Even satan's intrigues, craftiness, and schemes are exposed in these courts: *"Nothing in all creation is hidden from God's sight. Everything is uncovered and laid bare before the eyes of Him to whom we must give account"* (Heb. 4:13). Examples of this court system are seen in Zechariah chapter 3 and Daniel chapter 7.

This court system is all-powerful in accordance with the nature of the Judge of the universe. This court system stands above and towers over the corruptive and manipulative justice system of this perishing world. Biblical examples abound and together with the countless real-life experiences of this system, we see glimpses of a truly divine system that offers us clues as to how a perfect justice can actually operate in an imperfect earth.

BIBLICAL EXAMPLES OF COURT-LIKE DREAMS AND VISIONS

Laban Summoned to the Court of God

Dreamer and the Dream	God's Verdict
Laban didn't learn of their flight for three days. Then, taking several men with him, he set out in hot pursuit and caught up with them seven days later, at Mount Gilead (Gen. 31:22-23).	VERDICT *That night God appeared in a dream,* **"Watch out what you say to Jacob,"** *he was told.* **"Don't give him your blessing and don't curse him"** (Gen. 31:22-24 TLB).

King Abimelech Acquitted in God's Court

Dreamer and the Dream

Now Abraham moved on from there into the region of the Negev and lived between Kadesh and Shur. For a while he stayed in Gerar, and there Abraham said of his wife Sarah, "She is my sister." Then Abimelech king of Gerar sent for Sarah and took her (Gen. 20:1-2).

God's Verdict

VERDICT

But God came to Abimelech in a dream one night and said to him, "You are as good as dead because of the woman you have taken; she is a married woman" (Gen. 20:3).

DEFENSE

Now Abimelech had not gone near her, so he said, "Lord, will you destroy an innocent nation? Did he not say to me, 'She is my sister,' and didn't she also say, 'He is my brother'? I have done this with a clear conscience and clean hands" (Gen. 20:4-5).

VERDICT

Then God said to him in the dream, "Yes, I know you did this with a clear conscience, and so I have kept you from sinning against me. That is why I did not let you touch her. Now return the man's wife, for he is a prophet, and he will pray for you and you will live. But if you do not return her, you may be sure that you and all yours will die" (Gen. 20:6-7).

PETER'S MINDSET CORRECTED IN THE COURT OF GOD

Vision and Recipient	God's Verdict
About noon the following day as they were on their journey and approaching the city, Peter went up on the roof to pray. He became hungry and wanted something to eat, and while the meal was being prepared, he fell into a trance. He saw heaven opened and something like a large sheet being let down to earth by its four corners. It contained all kinds of four-footed animals, as well as reptiles of the earth and birds of the air (Acts 10:9-12).	**COMMAND** *Then a voice told him, "Get up, Peter. Kill and eat"* (Acts 10:13).

DEFENSE

"Surely not, Lord!" Peter replied. "I have never eaten anything impure or unclean" (Acts 10:14).

This happened three times, and immediately the sheet was taken back to heaven. While Peter was wondering about the meaning of the vision, the men sent by Cornelius found out where Simon's house was and stopped at the gate. They called out, asking if Simon who was known as Peter was staying there. While Peter was still thinking about the vision, the Spirit said to him, "Simon, three men are looking for you. So get up and go downstairs. Do not hesitate to go with them, for I have sent them" (Acts 10:16-20).

VERDICT

The voice spoke to him a second time, "Do not call anything impure that God has made clean" (Acts 10:15).

POINTS TO NOTE

- Edicts from these courts with God should not be contravened because any such violation carries dire consequences. King Abimelech would have died if he had ignored the verdict from his encounter with God.

- Many people regularly receive court-like audiences with God in their nightly encounters and it is important to know how to handle these verdicts that may emanate from these courts.

- It is important that we are truthful in handling the verdicts because nothing is hidden before God.

POINTS TO PONDER

1. Studying examples of how dreams were interpreted in the Bible is instructive, thoroughly interesting, and helpful in understanding the mysteries of God. Special anointing actually lifts off the pages of the Bible. Such impartation sharpens and seasons your mind and sets the stage for future godly interpretation. Have you found this to be true?

   _____

   _____

2. As you studied some of the classic examples in this chapter, was your confidence built up? Are you ready to make meaning out of the dreams you receive?

   _____

   _____

3. Which example(s) spoke to your heart most loudly? Think about why this special connection was made and what possible meaning(s) it may have for you.

   _____

   _____

Chapter 8

DREAMS VERSUS VISIONS

WAS IT A DREAM OR A VISION?

IN THIS SHORT CHAPTER, I discuss those spiritual experiences that are hard to define as whether you have experienced a dream or a vision. It is important to note that some dreams can contain visions and some visions may contain dream experiences. Examples:

- Vision in a dream. *"In the first year of Belshazzar king of Babylon, Daniel had a dream, and visions passed through his mind as he was lying on his bed. He wrote down the substance of his dream"* (Dan. 7:1).

- Dream within the context of a vision. *"As the sun was setting, Abram fell into a deep sleep, and a thick and dreadful darkness came over him"* (Gen. 15:12).

VISIONS WHILE AWAKE

When a vision is experienced by a group of people, commonly the people within the group perceive the vision at different levels, mostly according to the various levels of their spiritual visual acuity and also according to the sovereign choice of God for each person. The Damascus road experience is a good example of this circumstance.

*Meanwhile, Saul was still breathing out murderous threats against the Lord's disciples. He went to the high priest and asked him for letters to the synagogues in Damascus, so that if he found any there who belonged to the Way, whether men or women, he might take them as prisoners to Jerusalem. As he neared Damascus on his journey, suddenly a light from heaven flashed around him. He fell to the ground and heard a voice say to him, "Saul, Saul, why do you persecute Me?" "Who are You, Lord?" Saul asked. "I am Jesus, whom you are persecuting," he replied. "Now get up and go into the city, and you will be told what you must do." **The men traveling with Saul stood there speechless; they heard the sound but did not see anyone.** Saul got up from the ground, but when he opened his eyes he could see nothing. So they led him by the hand into Damascus. For three days he was blind, and did not eat or drink anything* (Acts 9:1-9).

This also happens with most angelic corporal appearances:

*At that time I, Daniel, mourned for three weeks. I ate no choice food; no meat or wine touched my lips; and I used no lotions at all until the three weeks were over. On the twenty-fourth day of the first month, as I was standing on the bank of the great river, the Tigris, I looked up and there before me was a man dressed in linen, with a belt of the finest gold round his waist. His body was like chrysolite, his face like lightning, his eyes like flaming torches, his arms and legs like the gleam of burnished bronze, and his voice like the sound of a multitude. **I, Daniel, was the only one who saw the vision; the men with me did not see it, but such terror overwhelmed them that they fled and hid themselves. So I was left alone, gazing at this great vision;** I had no strength left, my face turned deathly pale and I was helpless. Then I heard him speaking, and as I listened to him, I fell into a deep sleep, my face to the ground* (Daniel 10:2-9).

Sometimes there is full view for all recipients of the corporate vision such as the mysterious handwriting on the wall or other apparitions that can be seen with natural eyes.

Suddenly, as they were drinking from these cups, **they saw the fingers of a man's hand writing on the plaster of the wall opposite the lampstand.** *The king himself saw the fingers as they wrote. His face blanched with fear and such terror gripped him that his knees knocked together and his legs gave way beneath him* (Daniel 5:4-6 TLB).

DREAMS WHILE ASLEEP

On the other hand, dreams are only received when the person is asleep and therefore involve only the spirit of the dreamer. Mind and body participation in dreams reception is highly restricted. Therefore in most cases what appears to be bodily involvement in dream reception is probably because of the visions within the dreams.

Apart from the differences cited between dreams and visions, there are other key differences:

DIFFERENCES BETWEEN DREAMS AND VISIONS

To receive dreams, the mind has to be asleep; see Genesis 15:12-13.	Visions are received with varying degrees of mind alertness.
Dreams are always experienced on a personal basis.	Visions can be experienced in a group setting.
Dreams are received by the spirit of man; are mostly spirit-to-spirit encounters.	Visions may involve varying degrees of the physical or natural realm, such as tangible bodily experiences.
Dreams are more symbolic.	Visions are more literal.

And it shall come to pass in the last days, God declares, that I will pour out My Spirit upon all mankind, and your sons and daughters shall prophesy [telling forth the divine counsels] and your young men shall see visions (divinely granted appearances) and your old men shall dreams [divinely suggested] dreams (Acts 2:17 AMP).

133

Here, the Amplified Bible refers to *vision* as divinely granted appearances and *dreams* as divinely suggested communications. In other words, dreams are more suggested possibilities than inevitabilities. Dreams of promises need to be prayed through for fulfillment. Whereas dreams of warning need to be prayed through so the danger can be averted.

> *he said, "Listen to my words: 'When a prophet of the Lord is among you, I reveal Myself to him in visions, I speak to him in dreams'"* (Numbers 12:6).

Here the writer of Numbers seems to indicate that God reveals His divine attributes such as awesomeness, majesty, color or lights in a vision and He speaks to man in dreams. *To speak* suggests close intimacy and more of a heart-to-heart connection. God commonly connects with a dreamer's heart in dreams.

POINTS TO PONDER

1. Dreams are only received when you are asleep and therefore involve only your spirit. Mind and body participation in dreams reception is highly restricted. Therefore in most cases what appears to be bodily involvement in dream reception is probably because of the visions within the dreams. Have you experienced a vision within a dream?

2. The Amplified Bible refers to *vision* as divinely granted appearances and *dreams* as divinely suggested communications. How do you distinguish dreams from visions?

3. What does it mean to you that "God commonly connects with a dreamer's heart in dreams"?

PART II

VISIONS

Chapter 9

VISIONS OF THE
SUPERNATURAL

A VISION IS THE VISUAL reception of revelation or visual perception of a supernatural event—usually perceived by spiritual eyes. The Amplified Bible refers to visions as divinely granted appearances, *"And it shall come to pass in the last days, God declares, that I will pour out My Spirit upon all mankind, and your sons and daughters shall prophesy [telling forth the divine counsels] and your young men shall see visions (divinely granted appearances) and your old men shall dreams [divinely suggested] dreams"* (Acts 2:17 AMP).

One inference from this is that as Christians we should not seek after visions as many non-Christians do. Many do this in the name of "visionary quest." But we should seek after God realizing that it is at God's initiative that spiritual experiences—including visions—are *divinely granted*.

Visions are usually seen with spiritual eyes. Visions encompass a wide spectrum of spiritual occurrences that have differing involvement of the natural realm and could involve the human body in tangible ways. There is great interplay between the supernatural and natural realms in most visionary encounters. In most cases this is not the same with pure dreams or dreams without visionary components.

When a visionary happening has sufficiently permeated the physical realm such that it becomes perceptible by the natural eyes, it is then called an *apparition*. The degree to which a person is able to perceive a visionary occurrence depends on

God and to a large extent is proportional to the spiritual visual acuity (ability to see into the spirit ream) of the person. Thus a person with well-matured spiritual acuity will be able to see a vision that other people are not able to see. This accounts for the variable perception of vision among the people receiving a corporate vision. For example, in the case of Elisha and his servant, Elisha's servant could not see the vision of the chariots of fire and the horses of fire around Elisha even though the prophet himself could see them. The prophet had a more mature spiritual visual acuity than his servant, among other factors. But the servant was subsequently able to see them when the prophet Elisha prayed for him and his spiritual eyes opened. Prayers instantly and divinely increased his spiritual visual acuity.

VISIONARY APPEARANCES

Visionary appearances can take various forms, ranging from those with a significant auditory perception component, such as the one that young Samuel had during the time of his tutelage under Eli: *"Samuel lay down until morning and then opened the doors of the house of the Lord. He was afraid to tell Eli **the vision**"* (1 Sam. 3:15). There are the uncommon ones such as the transfiguration of Jesus: *"Now as they came down from the mountain, Jesus commanded them saying "**tell the vision** to no one until the son of Man is risen from the dead"* (Matt. 17:9). And also there are the life transforming ones like the one that Paul experienced on his way to Damascus.

Various forms of visions have been used to call people to action:

- Encouraging visions; Genesis 46:1-5.
- Visions with significant auditory component; 1 Samuel 3:10-15.
- A call to action; the Macedonian call; Acts 16:6-10.
- Warning vision; Acts 18:9, Acts 22:17-21.
- Life-transforming vision; Paul's experience on the way to Damascus; Acts 9:3-9.
- A call to destiny; Moses' burning bush experience; Exodus 3:1-10.
- Visions of divine judgment; the mysterious hand writing on the wall (apparitions); Daniel 5:5-7.
- Trances, a twilight state; Acts 10:9-17.

- Third heaven experiences; 2 Corinthians 12:1-5.

To properly understand dreams and visions, one has to examine them within the context of the bigger picture of the interaction between the earth and the heavens or between the supernatural and the natural realms. At the time of creation, God made the heavens and the earth at the same time: *"In the beginning God created the heavens and the earth"* (Gen. 1:1).

So right from the start, there is a constant connection between the third heaven and the earth. In this divine partnership between the third heaven and the earth, called *the universe*, the heaven is invisible to the natural eyes and the earth is the visible and tangible part of the partnership.

Broadly, dreams and visions are the visual perception of the supernatural world from our earthly abode; and on the other hand, visitation of celestial beings to the earth like angelic visitations represent one of the ways the supernatural world breaks into our earthly world. These occurrences need to break through the intervening interface of a celestial expanse called the second heaven.

The *second heaven* is the celestial expanse immediately hovering and covering the earth but beneath the third heaven. The *third heaven* is the abode of God and home of the departed saints of God. The earth is the terrestrial expanse where the wind blows, the birds fly, the sun shines, and the clouds move—this is the expanse where we live.

An *open heaven* is when the covering of the second heaven over the earth is opened up to establish connection between the earth and the third heaven breaking through the second heaven interface. The third heaven is the highest level of revelatory experience.

HEAVENLY ACTIVITIES ON EARTH

The common manifestation when the third heaven opens upon the earth is divine revelations. Other benefits include material and immaterial blessings. The third heaven has doors and windows through which we can access and receive from the spirit realm.

Windows, Doors, and Gate of the Third Heaven

The Scriptures speak of the doors, windows, and gate of heaven:

> *"Bring the whole tithe into the storehouse, so that there may be food in My house, and test Me now in this," says the Lord of host, "if I will not open for you* **the windows of heaven** *and pour out for you a blessing until it overflows"* (Malachi 3:10 NASB).

> *The officer on whose arm the king was leaning said to the man of God, "Look, even if the Lord should open the floodgates* [windows] *of the heavens, could this happen?"* (2 Kings 7:2).

Judgment from the windows of heaven:

> *And after the seven days the floodwaters came on the earth. In the six hundredth year of Noah's life, on the seventeenth day of the second month—on that day all the springs of the great deep burst forth, and the* **floodgates** [windows] **of the heavens** *were opened. And rain fell on the earth forty days and forty nights. On that very day Noah and his sons, Shem, Ham and Japheth, together with his wife and the wives of his three sons, entered the ark. They had with them every wild animal according to its kind, all livestock according to their kinds, every creature that moves along the ground according to its kind and every bird according to its kind, everything with wings* (Genesis 7:10-14).

> *After this I looked, and there before me was* **a door standing open** *in heaven. And the voice I had first heard speaking to me like a trumpet said, "Come up here, and I will show you what must take place after this"* (Revelation 4:1).

> *He was afraid and said, "How awesome is this place! This is none other than the house of God; this is the* **gate of heaven"** (Genesis 28:17).

Note that the Bible says that the house of God is the gate of heaven. In other words, a good house of God is a good gate of heaven to the people. I believe this is why most people find it easier to gain entrance to the heavenly realm on a corporate basis as we worship in the house of God.

Another common manifestation of open heaven is the free flow of the eternal Word of God and availability of the mighty hand of God to perform miracles, wonders, or strange events:

> *In the thirtieth year, in the fourth month on the fifth day, while I was among the exiles by the Kebar River, the heavens were opened and I saw visions of God. On the fifth of the month—it was the fifth year of the exile of King Jehoiachin—the word of the Lord came to Ezekiel the priest, the son of Buzi, by the Kebar River in the land of the Babylonians. There the hand of the Lord was upon him* (Ezekiel 1:1-3).

Visions of the Heavenly Realm

We can categorize the interactions between the third heaven and the earth into two broad groups—actual and visual experiences—and whether it is the third heaven that breaks into the earth realm or it is an interaction beginning from the earth into the heaven. However, every genuine spiritual experience should be at the initiative of God Himself, or else it is counterfeit.

When God allows humankind to peep into the supernatural realm from the natural realm, these experiences are most of the time visual, with a few rare actual experiences. These experiences include:

- Dreams
- Visions
- Translation
- Throne room encounters:
- Visual experience; Isaiah 6:1
- Actual experience; 2 Corinthians 12:1-4

Broadly speaking, when the supernatural realm breaks into the natural realm, the experiences are varied and could be either visual or actual. Most of these experiences include:

Apparitions

- Fourth man in the burning furnace
- Angelic appearances

Divine sight

- The burning bush experience

Visitation by celestial beings

- Angelic visitations
- Jesus Christ appearing to disciples on the road to Emmaus
- Visitations from the realms of hell

Strange and mysterious events

- The hand writing on the wall
- Wrestling with the angel of the Lord as Jacob did
- Transfiguration of Jesus Christ

CO-EXISTENT REALM OF THE SPIRITUAL REALM

The story of Elisha and his servant, when the Assyrian army surrounded them, is a good case to illustrate the reality of the co-existence and interaction of the spiritual and the natural realms. Their experience is recorded in the Bible:

When the servant of the man of God got up and went out early the next morning, an army with horses and chariots had surrounded the city. "Oh, my lord, what shall we do?" the servant asked. "Don't be afraid," the prophet answered. "Those who are with us are more than those who are with them." And Elisha prayed, "O Lord, open his eyes *so that he may see." Then the Lord opened the servant's eyes, and he looked and **saw the hills full of horses and chariots of fire all round Elisha**. As the enemy came down toward him, Elisha prayed to the Lord, "Strike these people with blindness." So He struck them with blindness, as Elisha had asked* (2 Kings 6:15-18).

What we must realize is that those *"horses and chariots of fire"* existed even before Elisha prayed, though his servant could not see them at the time with his natural eyes. These chariots were actually present though they were only visible to spiritual eyes. These were celestial beings visiting the earth realm.

In this instance, God allowed Elisha's servant to peep into and have sight of what exists in the realm of the spirit. However, notice that he could not see them until his spiritual eyes were opened. Visions are seen with spiritual eyes. Notice also the experience, though predominantly visual for Elisha's servant, was an actual experience, which means it was the reality of what was happening at the time. In this story, we see actual visitation of celestial beings as well as the opening of spiritual eyes by God so that the servant of Elisha could see them.

Steps to Correct Interpretation

One should not advocate a formula-based approach to dream interpretation. Reliance on the Holy Spirit is an absolute necessity. However, I have found the following to be helpful in my teaching program.

- Wait for the prompting of the Holy Spirit. Correct interpretation does not come by human reasoning, but by an inflow into our hearts or subconscious from God.
- Understand the meaning of the symbols and actions.
- Explain the relevance of events and symbols to the dreamer's circumstance.

Be sure to always put together a possible storyline for the dream. The plot should assemble the dream's elements and events without any contradiction. What follows is helpful in determining whether the storyline is correct:

- All elements will agree with or fit into the plot.

- All actions will fit into the context of the plot.

- If only one or two elements do not fit with the plot while the majority of others are in agreement, then the derived "meaning" of the symbol is not the appropriate one. Therefore, check other meanings of the symbol. If more than two elements don't fit into the plot, then be sure to review it.

For more information see *Dreams and Visions Volume 1* by Dr. Joe Ibojie

POINTS TO PONDER

1. Visions are usually seen with spiritual eyes and encompass a wide spectrum of spiritual occurrences that have differing involvement of the natural realm and could involve the human body in tangible ways. Have you noticed (or do you expect to notice) that here is great interplay between the supernatural and natural realms in most visionary encounters?

    _____

    _____

2. The *second heaven* is the celestial expanse immediately hovering and covering the earth. The *third heaven* is the abode of God and home of the departed saints of God. An *open heaven* is when the covering of the second heaven over the earth is opened up to establish connection between the earth and the third heaven breaking through the second heaven interface. How familiar are you with these spiritual realms? Why is it important to understand these realms?

    _____

    _____

3. What is the most astounding aspect of the story of Elisha and his servant? How would you describe the reality of the co-existence and interaction of the spiritual and the natural realms based on this biblical example?

    _____

    _____

Chapter 10

VISIONS AND
THE THIRD HEAVEN

THOUGH INVISIBLE, the third heaven is as real as the visible and tangible earth in which we live. There are constant interactions between the earth and the third heaven. These interactions can be enhanced or clouded. Also, things we do in the natural world can either hinder the connection or enhance communication. In the Book of Deuteronomy, we are told that disobedience to God's commandments can block this communication.

> *And your heavens, which are over your head, shall be bronze; the earth, which is under you, shall be iron* (Deuteronomy 28:23).

In this instance in the Bible, God described the heavens over a person's head as the accessibility of the third heaven through the piercing of the second heaven interface by the person. By sovereignty, God can decide to enhance the connection or to blanket this communication between the earth and third heaven, as the patriarch Jacob experienced on his way to Haran (see Gen. 28:10-17).

In the New Testament, Jesus Christ described the essence of New Testament teaching on the concept of open heavens. John 1:49-51 says, "Nathanael answered and said to Him, 'Rabbi, You are the Son of God! You are the King of Israel!' Jesus answered and said to him, 'Because I said to you, "I saw you under the fig tree," do you believe? You will see greater things than these.' And He said to him, 'Most assuredly, I say to you, hereafter you shall see heaven open, and the angels of God ascending and descending upon the Son of Man.'" Indeed, by the death of Jesus the veil to the most holy place was torn; and by His resurrection, access to the heavens was established. This is without geographical limitation or time restriction! The key requirements are salvation and faith in Jesus; then access to the heavens is granted and built upon Jesus.

OPEN HEAVEN AND HEAVENLY PORTALS

As mentioned briefly in previous chapters, an open heaven is when the covering of the second heaven over the earth is opened up to establish a connection between the earth and the third heaven over a place. In other words, an opening of the heavens is the bypassing of the hindrances of the second heaven to connect the third heaven—God's abode—with the earth. The openness or the manifestations of the third heaven over a place can be temporary or permanent. Temporary openness can be periodic or can be accentuated. When the third heaven opens over a place on a permanent basis, it is called a *heavenly portal.*

John Paul Jackson, a pioneer in scriptural understanding of dreams, defines a heavenly portal as a *"spherical opening of light that offers divine protection by which angels and heavenly beings can come and go, without demonic interference. God has designed portals to begin in third Heaven, travel through the second heaven and open upon Earth."[1]* This definition amply gives a working background and proper context for understanding of this rather fascinating subject.

A heavenly portal is a doorway of the third heaven, cutting through the covering of the second heaven and breaking open upon the earth. This doorway is a permanent connection between the first heaven and the third heaven. It originates from God and comes with divine insurance for the permanence of the connection. However, the actions of men on earth and demonic activities can influence the intensity of the traffic in this connection. Because of the permanent openness of third heaven upon the earth in these places, these portals are usually areas of high spiritual contention between the devil, his cohorts, and godly agents. The Bible is replete with instances of abuse and misuse of these places. Ignorantly, unchristian men have frequently used such portals as places to go to seek God's power by ungodly means. Others have used portals as places to go for visionary quest, idolatry practices, and ritualistic activities. Most high places in the Bible were built around the premise of easy accessibility of the heavenly realm in these places—portals.

At the heavenly portal in Bethel, Jacob's spiritual eyes were opened, and he saw the traffic of angels ascending and descending on a ladder connecting the earth and the third heaven. He also saw God at the heavenly end of the ladder. In this encounter, God conferred Abraham's blessing on Jacob. This all came to Jacob in a dream of the night.

> *When Jacob awoke from his sleep, he thought, "Surely the Lord is in this place, and I was not aware of it." He was afraid and said, "How awesome is this place! This is none other than the house of God; **this is the gate of heaven.**" Early the next morning Jacob took the stone he had placed under his head and set it up as a pillar and poured oil on top of it. He called that place Bethel, though the city used to be called Luz. Then Jacob made a vow, saying, "If God will be with me and will watch over me on this journey I am taking and will give me food to eat and clothes to wear so that I return safely to my father's house, then the Lord will be my God and this stone that I have set up as a pillar will be God's house, and of all that you give me I will give You a tenth"* (Genesis 28:16-22).

At the end of this awesome encounter, Jacob concluded the place was the gate of heaven or a doorway to heaven, in other words *he called it a portal*. From this experience, we may infer that in a portal there is traffic from heaven of angelic beings, blessings, impartation, and revelation. We can say Jacob had revelation during the encounter because he said, *"Surely, the Lord is this place, I do not know it."* It is also from this point that the Bible started to speak of God as the God of Abraham, Isaac, and Jacob; a portal is therefore a place where a life can be transformed and realigned to godly purposes and channeled toward its destiny by godly impartation.

The devil always seeks to influence the portal. First, he attempts to possess the traffic on the pathway for his evil watchman activities. Second, he would try to oppress and pollute human activities in this place. The devil's desire is to control how man uses or misuses the place. And ultimately the devil seeks to establish demonic practices in these places. However, all of the misuse and abuse by satan and man are equally reversible when men take appropriate steps to move toward God. The portal can become sanctified and consecrated once again to God.

There are many examples of portals in the Bible. Some of the ancient portals identified in biblical times follow.

Bethel—the house of God and the gate of heaven

- Bethel is the site of Abraham's altar to God's covenant. A citadel of prayers: *"From there he went on toward the hills east of Bethel and pitched his tent, with Bethel on the west and Ai on the east. There he built an altar to the Lord and called on the name of the Lord"* (Gen. 12:8).

- Bethel is a place of covenant, a place of trust in God, a place of the abiding presence of God; and the place where Abraham returned to time and time again: *"So Abram went up from Egypt to the Negev, with his wife and everything he had, and Lot went with him. Abram had become very wealthy in livestock and in silver and gold. From the Negev he went from place to place until he came to Bethel, to the place between Bethel and Ai where his tent had been earlier and where he had first built an altar. There Abram called on the name of the Lord"* (Gen. 13:1-4).

- Bethel is where Jacob erected a pillar to mark his dream as a holy sanctuary of God; see Genesis 28:10-22.

- Bethel is a place of memorial and purity; a place God Himself directed Jacob to settle in: *"Then God said to Jacob, 'Go up to Bethel and settle there, and build an altar there to God, who appeared to you when you were fleeing from your brother Esau.' So Jacob said to his household and to all who were with him, 'Get rid of the foreign gods you have with you, and purify yourselves and change your clothes. Then come, let us go up to Bethel, where I will build an altar to God, who answered me in the day of my distress and who has been with me wherever I have gone.' So they gave Jacob all the foreign gods they had and the rings in their ears, and Jacob buried them under the oak at Shechem. Then they set out, and the terror of God fell upon the towns all around them so that no one pursued them. Jacob and all the people with him came to Luz (that is, Bethel) in the land of Canaan. There he built an altar, and he called the place El Bethel, because it was there that God revealed Himself to him when he was fleeing from his brother"* (Gen. 35:1-7).

- Bethel is a place of blessings, realignment, transformation, and a place Jacob returned to meet with God: *"After Jacob returned from Paddan Aram, God appeared to him again and blessed him. God said to him, 'Your name is Jacob, but you will no longer be called Jacob; your name will be Israel.' So He named him Israel. And God said to him, 'I am God Almighty; be fruitful and increase in number. A nation and a community of nations will come from you, and kings will come from your body. The land I gave to Abraham and Isaac I also give to you, and I will give this land to your descendants after you.' Then God went up from him at the place where He had talked with him. Jacob set up a stone pillar at the place where God had talked with him, and he poured out a drink offering on it; he also poured oil on it. Jacob called the place where God had talked with him Bethel"* (Gen. 35:9-15).

- Bethel is place of high-level contention between good and evil forces; a place where King Jeroboam established a rival, idolatrous sanctuary to the temple at Jerusalem by setting up the golden calf: *"After seeking advice, the king made two golden calves. He said to the people, 'It is too much for you to go up to Jerusalem. Here are your gods, O Israel, who brought you up out of Egypt.' One he set up in Bethel, and the other in Dan. And this thing became a sin; the people went even as far as Dan to worship the one there. Jeroboam built shrines on high places and appointed priests from all sorts of people, even though they were not Levites"* (1 Kings 12:28-31).

- Bethel is later purged by King Josiah: *"Even the altar at Bethel, the high place made by Jeroboam son of Nebat, who had caused Israel to sin—even that altar and high place he demolished. He burned the high place and ground it to powder, and burned the Asherah pole also"* (2 Kings 23:15).

- Bethel is the present-day village of Beitin, twelve miles north of Jerusalem.

Mount Moriah—the mountain of God's provision

- Mount Moriah is a place of sacrifice; the place where Abraham attempted to offer Isaac as a sacrifice: *"Then God said, 'Take your son, your only son, Isaac, whom you love, and go to the region of Moriah. Sacrifice him there as a burnt offering on one of the mountains I will tell you about'"* (Gen. 22:2).

- Mount Moriah is a place of intimate moments with God; the Angel of the Lord called out to Abraham from heaven in an audible way: *"Then he reached out his hand and took the knife to slay his son. But the angel of the Lord called out to him from heaven, 'Abraham! Abraham!' 'Here I am,' he replied. 'Do not lay a hand on the boy,' he said. 'Do not do anything to him. Now I know that you fear God, because you have not withheld from me your son, your only son'"* (Gen. 22:10-12).

- Mount Moriah is a place of divine provision where perfection or completeness is demonstrated; called the mountain of God's provision: *"So Abraham called that place 'The Lord Will Provide.' And to this day it is said, 'On the mountain of the Lord it will be provided'"* (Gen. 22:14).

- Mount Moriah is a place travailing in prayers, a threshing floor, and the place that was purchased by King David from Araunah, the Jebusite: *"...On that day Gad went to David and said to him, 'Go up and build an altar to the Lord on the threshing-floor of Araunah the Jebusite'..."* (2 Sam. 24:16-25).

- Mount Moriah is a place of worship where King Solomon sited the temple when he centralized worship in Jerusalem: *"Then Solomon began to build the temple of the Lord in Jerusalem on Mount Moriah, where the Lord had appeared to his father David. It was on the threshing floor of Araunah the Jebusite, the place provided by David"* (2 Chron. 3:1).

- Mount Moriah is a place highly contested in the spirit; today the Islamic shrine known as the Dome of the Rock is situated at the top of Mount Moriah.

Gibeon—the great high place

- Gibeon is where the tabernacle meeting with God took place; a place where Moses erected the Tabernacle of Meeting, the old tent of Moses: *"and Solomon and the whole assembly went to the high place at Gibeon, for God's Tent of Meeting was there, which Moses the Lord's servant had made in the desert"* (2 Chron. 1:3).

- Gibeon is the official dwelling place of the Ark of God; a place where the Ark dwelt until it was captured by the Philistines: *"And Samuel's word came to all Israel. Now the Israelites went out to fight against the Philistines. The Israelites camped at Ebenezer, and the Philistines at Aphek. The Philistines deployed their forces to meet Israel, and as the battle spread, Israel was defeated by the Philistines, who killed about four thousand of them on the battlefield. When the soldiers returned to camp, the elders of Israel asked, 'Why did the Lord bring defeat upon us today before the Philistines? Let us bring the ark of the Lord's covenant from Shiloh, so that it may go with us and save us from the hand of our enemies.' So the people sent men to Shiloh, and they brought back the ark of the covenant of the Lord Almighty, who is enthroned between the cherubim. And Eli's two sons, Hophni and Phinehas, were there with the ark of the covenant of God. When the ark of the Lord's covenant came into the camp, all Israel raised such a great shout that the ground shook. Hearing the uproar, the Philistines asked, 'What's all this shouting in the Hebrew camp?' When they learned that the ark of the Lord had come into the camp, the Philistines were afraid. 'A god has come into the camp,' they said. 'We're in trouble! Nothing like this has happened before. Woe to us! Who will deliver us from the hand of these mighty gods? They are the gods who struck the Egyptians with all kinds of plagues in the desert. Be strong, Philistines! Be men, or you will be subject to the Hebrews, as they have been to you. Be men, and fight!' So the Philistines fought, and the Israelites were defeated and every man fled to his tent. The slaughter was very great; Israel lost thirty thousand foot soldiers. The ark of God was captured, and Eli's two sons, Hophni and Phinehas, died"* (1 Sam. 4:1-11).

- Gibeon is a place where King David constructed a tent for the Ark: *"David left Zadok the priest and his fellow priests before the tabernacle of the Lord at the high place in Gibeon"* (1 Chron. 16:39).

- Gibeon is the high place where King Solomon offered sacrifice unto God, where he had an interactive dream and he became endowed with divine wisdom: *"and Solomon and the whole assembly went to the high place at Gibeon, for God's Tent of Meeting was there, which Moses the Lord's servant had made in the desert. Now David had brought up the ark of God from Kiriath Jearim to the place he had prepared for it, because he had pitched a tent for it in Jerusalem. But the bronze altar that Bezalel son of Uri, the son of Hur, had made was in Gibeon in front of the tabernacle of the Lord; so Solomon and the assembly enquired of him there. Solomon went up to the bronze altar before the Lord in the Tent of Meeting and offered a thousand burnt offerings on it. That night God appeared to Solomon and said to him, 'Ask for whatever you want me to give you.' Solomon answered God, 'You have shown great kindness to David my father and have made me king in his place. Now, Lord God, let your promise to my father David be confirmed, for you have made me king over a people who are as numerous as the dust of the earth. Give me wisdom and knowledge, that I may lead this people, for who is able to govern this great people of yours?' God said to Solomon, 'Since this is your heart's desire and you have not asked for wealth, riches or honour, nor for the death of your enemies, and since you have not asked for a long life but for wisdom and knowledge to govern my people over whom I have made you king, therefore wisdom and knowledge will be given you. And I will also give you wealth, riches and honour, such as no king who was before you ever had and none after you will have'"* (2 Chron. 1:3-12).

Mount Sinai—God's holy mountain

- Mount Sinai is also called Mount Herob. This is one of the most outstanding heavenly portals in biblical times and one of the most sacred locations in Israel's history.

- Mount Sinai is the where Moses experienced the burning bush; a place of divine counter, of selfless, of sacrifice and of divine impartation; the spectacle of the burning bush that was not being consumed *"Now Moses was tending the flock of Jethro his father-in-law, the priest of Midian, and he led the flock to the far side of the desert and came to Horeb, the mountain of God. There the angel of the Lord appeared to him in flames of fire from within a bush. Moses saw that though the bush was on fire it did not burn up"* (Exod. 3:1-2).

- Mount Sinai is a place of hearing the rhema word of God; where God spoke to Elijah in a still small voice.

- Mount Sinai is where God gave Israel the Ten Commandments and guidance of right living; see Exodus 24:12-18.

- Mount Sinai is where the people of Israel learned the blessings of obedience and the tragic consequences of disobedience.

- Mount Sinai is the mountain where God said to Moses. *"when you have brought the people out of Egypt, you will worship God on this mountain"* (Exod. 3:12).

- Mount Sinai is the mountain where God asked Moses to consecrate the people but also to set bounds for the Israelites when they approach the mountain; see Exodus 19:10-15.

- Mount Sinai is the mountain where the entire people saw the Lord come down in thunder and lightning: *"On the morning of the third day there was thunder and lightning, with a thick cloud over the mountain, and a very loud trumpet blast. Everyone in the camp trembled (Exod. 19:16). And also in "The earth shook, the heavens poured down rain, before God, the One of Sinai, before God, the God of Israel"* (Ps. 68:8).

- Mount Sinai is where the reverent fear of the Lord was instilled in the people: *"When the people saw the thunder and lightning and heard the trumpet and saw the mountain in smoke, they trembled with fear. They stayed at a distance and said to Moses, 'Speak to us yourself and we will listen. But do not have God speak to us or we will die'"* (Exod. 20:18-19).

- Mount Sinai is where Moses met with God in a dark cloud: *"The people remained at a distance, while Moses approached the thick darkness where God was"* (Exod. 20:21).

- *"Then You came down on Mount Sinai and spoke with them from heaven; You gave them just ordinances and true laws, good statues and commandments"* (Neh. 9:13).

- Mount Sinai is where the people erected an altar and twelve pillars at the foot of the mountain; see Exodus 24:3-8.

Jerusalem—the city of God

- Jerusalem, the city of God, is a major heavenly portal on the earth. Jerusalem will become the seat of divine rulership on the earth.

- Jerusalem is the only city on earth upon which Jehovah placed His name: *"I will give one tribe to his son so that David My servant may always have a lamp before Me in Jerusalem, the city where I chose to put My Name"* (1 Kings 11:36).

- Jerusalem is the seat of divinely constituted government: *"Many nations will come and say, 'Come, let us go up to the mountain of the Lord, to the house of the God of Jacob. He will teach us his ways, so that we may walk in his paths.' The law will go out from Zion, the word of the Lord from Jerusalem"* (Micah 4:2).

- Jerusalem's portal is remarkable because it is the birthplace of the Church of Christ: *"When the day of Pentecost came, they were all together in one place. Suddenly a sound like the blowing of a violent wind came from heaven and filled the whole house where they were sitting. They saw what seemed to be tongues of fire that separated and came to rest on each of them. All of them were filled with the Holy Spirit and began to speak in other tongues as the Spirit enabled them. Now there were staying in Jerusalem God-fearing Jews from every nation under heaven"* (Acts 2:1-5).

- Jerusalem is the place of the New Jerusalem—the holy city: *"Then I saw a new heaven and a new earth, for the first heaven and the first earth had passed away, and there was no longer any sea. I saw the Holy City, the New Jerusalem, coming down out of heaven from God, prepared as a bride beautifully dressed for her husband. And I heard a loud voice from the throne saying, 'Now the dwelling of God is with men, and He will live with them. They will be His people, and God Himself will be with them and be their God'"* (Rev. 21:1-3).

UNDERSTANDING TEMPORARY HEAVENLY OPENINGS

The temporary opening of the third heaven over a location on the earth or over a person's head can be facilitated by what the person does. We can take deliberate actions to enhance the easy flow of divine revelations over a place. By *open heaven* we also mean the frequency and the clarity of revelations in a place. The frequency of receiving revelation and their clarity are reflective of the openness of the third heaven over the place.

Prayers and Fasting

About noon the following day as they were on their journey and approaching the city, Peter went up on the roof to pray. He became hungry and wanted something to eat, and while the meal was being prepared, **he fell into a trance. He saw heaven opened** *and something like a large sheet being let down to earth by its four corners* (Acts 10:9-11).

In this instance, Peter's prayers and fasting undoubtedly contributed to the sudden opening of the heaven upon him. There are other things we do on earth that can make God create a temporary bypass through the covering of the second heaven.

Other examples of temporary opening of heaven:

Right Standing With God

The prophet Ezekiel's right standing with God facilitated the opening of the heavens over him for the following encounter to occur. *"In the thirtieth year, in the fourth month on the fifth day, while I was among the exiles by the Kebar River,* **the heavens were opened and I saw visions of God"** (Ezek. 1:1).

Jesus' obedience and submission to the will of God enhanced the opening of the third heaven over Him. *"As soon as Jesus was baptized, he went up out of the water. At that moment **heaven was opened, and he saw the Spirit of God descending like a dove and lighting on him. And a voice from heaven said, "This is My Son, whom I love; with Him I am well pleased"** (Matt. 3:16-17).*

The Cry of the People

In the Book of Isaiah, the prophet Isaiah cried out that the Lord would tie open the heavens and come down; the genuine heart cry of the people enhances the openness. *"Oh, that You would rend the heavens and come down, that the mountains would tremble before You!* (Isa. 64:1).

Actions and Attitudes of the People

At another time, the prophet Isaiah experienced an open heaven that he associated with the year when King Uzziah died. The Bible does not say why Isaiah associated the open heaven with that time; perhaps it was because the kingdom had remarkable success in the infrastructures and the political, agricultural, and military machineries, that the people became spiritually blinded and more reliant on the worldly system rather than the arm of God—who gave the wisdom for the worldly successes.

> *God helped him [King Uzziah] against the Philistines and against the Arabs who lived in Gur Baal and against the Meunites. The Ammonites brought tribute to Uzziah, and his fame spread as far as the border of Egypt, because he had become very powerful. Uzziah built towers in Jerusalem at the Corner Gate, at the Valley Gate and at the angle of the wall, and he fortified them. He also built towers in the desert and dug many cisterns, because he had much livestock in the foothills and in the plain. He had people working his fields and vineyards in the hills and in the fertile lands, for he loved the soil. Uzziah had a well-trained army, ready to go out by divisions according to their numbers as mustered by Jeiel the secretary and Maaseiah the officer under the direction of Hananiah, one of the royal officials. The total number of family leaders over the fighting men was 2,600.*

Under their command was an army of 307,500 men trained for war, a powerful force to support the king against his enemies. Uzziah provided shields, spears, helmets, coats of armour, bows and slingstones for the entire army. In Jerusalem he made machines designed by skilful men for use on the towers and on the corner defences to shoot arrows and hurl large stones. His fame spread far and wide, for he was greatly helped until he became powerful. But after Uzziah became powerful, his pride led to his downfall. He was unfaithful to the Lord his God, and entered the temple of the Lord to burn incense on the altar of incense (2 Chronicles 26:7-16).

It is possible that when King Uzziah died, there was a significant paradigm shift in the minds of the people, at least in the mind of prophet Isaiah, to begin to rely on the arms of God; as a result there was an enhanced openness of the heavens over him.

In the year that King Uzziah died, I saw the Lord seated on a throne, high and exalted, and the train of his robe filled the temple. Above him were seraphs, each with six wings: With two wings they covered their faces, with two they covered their feet, and with two they were flying (Isaiah 6:1-2).

Temporary opening of the heaven over a place can simply be an act of God as we see in Jacob's experience on his way to Haran; the heavens opened upon him and he saw a vision of a ladder from earth to heaven.

PREPARING TO RECEIVE REVELATIONS IN AN OPEN-HEAVEN ATMOSPHERE

Over the years, I have personally noticed both periods of intense revelatory reception and periods when revelations from God are rare. Also that there are things that could either diminish or increase the ability to receive revelations. The potential to receive is the giftedness, but the quantity and quality of what we receive is dependent on our walk and intimacy with God, for God confides in those who fear Him.

Let us look at the things that we can do to enhance our ability to receive in an open heaven situation.

- Intimacy with God

  For the perverse are an abomination [extremely disgusting and detestable] to the Lord; but His confidential communion and secret counsel are with the [uncompromisingly] righteous, (those who are upright and in right standing with Him) (Proverbs 3:32 AMP).

  The Lord confides in those who fear Him; He makes His covenant known to them (Psalm 25:14).

- Exercising spiritual senses

  But solid food is for the mature, who by constant use have trained themselves to distinguish good from evil (Hebrews 5:14).

This is particularly important, because to a very large extent, understanding what we receive from God is a studied art that could be made sharper by exercise. If we pay due attention to what we receive and seek the face of God, we get godly interpretation of our revelations. The more we use our spiritual senses, the sharper the understanding of spiritual things. Good understanding leads to appropriate response. Appropriate response to what God is doing in heaven leads to further release of revelations from Him.

- Being Bible-guided in our spiritual life

  As we see in the Book of Deuteronomy, the heavens over a place can become inaccessible if the people live in disobedience to God. *"And your heavens, which are over your head, shall be bronze; the earth, which is under you, shall be iron"* (Deut. 28:23).

- Strengthening the spirit man

  I keep asking that the God of our Lord Jesus Christ, the glorious Father, may give you the Spirit of wisdom and revelation, so that you may know Him better. I pray also that the eyes of your heart may be enlightened in order that you may know the hope to which He has called you, the riches of His glorious inheritance in the saints, and His incomparably great power for us who believe... (Ephesians 1:17-19).

A man is only as strong as his spirit is. The strength of your spirit man reflects the quality of your relationship with God. A good and quality relationship with God makes a strong spirit man. A strong spirit receives clearly and abundantly from God. *I define the strength of the spirit man as one's ability to bear witness with the Spirit of God.* You receive more revelation if your spirit bears proper witness with the Spirit of God. You are able to recognize the prompting of God, and also are able to discern that which is godly and that which is not.

- Having a consistent and effective prayer life

  *if my people, who are called by My name, will humble themselves and pray and seek My face and turn from their wicked ways, then will I hear **from heaven and will forgive their sin** and will heal their land* (2 Chronicles 7:14).

  The king went to Gibeon to offer sacrifices, for that was the most important high place, and Solomon offered a thousand burnt offerings on that altar. At Gibeon the Lord appeared to Solomon during the night in a dream, and God said, "Ask for whatever you want me to give you" (1 Kings 3:4-5).

  About noon the following day as they were on their journey and approaching the city, Peter went up on the roof to pray. He became hungry and wanted something to eat, and while the meal was being prepared, he fell into a trance. He saw heaven opened and something like a large sheet being let down to earth by its four corners (Acts 10:9-11).

No man is stronger than his prayer life. If you have a good prayer life, you will receive wonderful revelatory encounters with God.

- Fasting

Fasting breaks the hold of the outer man and allows the inner man to manifest expressly. As the prophet Isaiah says:

Is this not the fast that I have chosen?
*To loose **the bonds of wickedness;***
*To undo **the heavy burdens;***
*To let the **oppressed go free;***
*And that you break **every yoke*** (Isaiah 58:6).

These are the things that thicken the outer man as your outer man out of necessity interacts with the world. Unless the outer man is broken, the inner spirit man will remain unexpressed: *"The Holy Spirit was showing by this that the way into the Most Holy Place had not yet been disclosed as long as the first tabernacle was still standing"* (Heb. 9:8).

When the inner man is fully manifest, the person is better able to receive and relate to God.

- Giving tithes and offerings

He and all his family were devout and God-fearing; he gave generously to those in need and prayed to God regularly. One day at about three in the afternoon, he had a vision. He distinctly saw an angel of God who came to him and said, "Cornelius!" Cornelius stared at him in fear. "What is it, Lord?" he asked. The angel answered, "Your prayers and gifts to the poor have come up as a memorial offering before God (Acts 10:2-4).

King Solomon's one night encounter in the court of God illustrates this principle very well. *"The king went to Gibeon to offer sacrifices, for that was the most important high place, and Solomon offered a thousand burnt offerings on that altar. **At Gibeon the Lord appeared to Solomon during the night in a dream**, and God said, 'Ask for whatever you want me to give you'"* (1 Kings 3:4-5).

And in the Book of Malachi, God said, *"Bring the whole tithe into the store house, so that there may be food in My house, and test Me now in this,' says the Lord of host, 'if I will not **open for you the window of heaven** and pour out for you a blessing until it overflows'"* (Mal. 3:10 NASB).

When the window of heaven is opened, not only physical blessings are released, there is increase of revelation from God and enhanced ability to receive from Him.

- Meditating on the Word of God

  And we have the word of the prophets made more certain, and you will do well to pay attention to it, as to a light shining in a dark place, until the day dawns and the morning star rises in your hearts" (2 Peter 1:19).

As the Bible says, the entrance of the Word brings light. When a person is well-grounded in the Word of God, revelations will not only increase, revelations will be received with great clarity. We should stand firm and hold onto the promises of God until we see the hope of God rise in our hearts.

- Staying in the place of your calling or responsibility

  And there were shepherds living out in the fields nearby, keeping watch over their flock at night. An angel of the Lord appeared to them... (Luke 2:8-9).

Though we are not quite sure why God chose to reveal this great news to these shepherds, we are sure of one thing, they were at their post of responsibility watching over their flock at night. And while in this post of responsibility, they were able to receive this great revelation.

ENDNOTE

1. John Paul Jackson, Streams Ministries e-letter, posted on the November 9, 2005.

POINTS TO PONDER

1. Though invisible, the third heaven is as real as the visible and tangible earth in which you live. There are constant interactions between the earth and the third heaven. These interactions can be enhanced or clouded. Are you enhancing or making cloudy your interaction with the third heaven?

---

2. A heavenly portal originates from God and comes with divine insurance for the permanence of the connection. However, the actions of people on earth and demonic activities can influence the intensity of the traffic in this connection. What activities do you think would create a portal traffic jam?

---

3. The more you use your spiritual senses, the sharper the understanding of spiritual things. Good understanding leads to appropriate response. Appropriate response to what God is doing in Heaven leads to further release of revelations from Him. Are you putting your spiritual senses to work?

Chapter 11

A CLOSED HEAVEN

A CLOSED HEAVEN is a non-permanent inaccessibility of the third heaven over a place. Closed heaven happens when access to the third heaven is temporarily blanketed over a place, such that people have no easy access to the third heaven. This situation is also called *brass heaven*. Though there are areas of permanent opening of the third heaven known as *heavenly portals*, there are no areas on earth that are permanently closed to the third heaven. Any areas closed to the third heaven can be reversed if men take the appropriate steps in response and obedience to God.

In Scripture, we can recognize two types of closed heaven situations: first on an *individual* level better known as the "silence of God." Such as the Bible says, *"And I will break and humble your pride in your power, and I will make your heavens as iron [yielding no answer, no blessings, no rain] and your earth [as sterile] as brass* (Lev. 26:19 AMP).

This of course refers to the consequences of individual sins in a person's life.

The other type of closed heaven is on a *corporate* level over a place as the Bible says in the following passages:

> *"The days are coming," declares the Sovereign Lord, "when I will send a famine through the land—not a famine of food or a thirst for water, but a famine of hearing the words of the Lord. Men will stagger from*

sea to sea and wander from north to east, searching for the word of the Lord, but they will not find it" (Amos 8:11-12).

The boy Samuel ministered before the Lord under Eli. **In those days the word of the Lord was rare; there were not many visions** (1 Samuel 3:1).

Her gates have sunk into the ground; their bars he has broken and destroyed. Her king and her princes are exiled among the nations, the law is no more, and **her prophets no longer find visions from the Lord** (Lamentations 2:9).

Be stunned and amazed, blind yourselves and be sightless; be drunk, but not from wine, stagger, but not from beer. **The Lord has brought over you a deep sleep: He has sealed your eyes (the prophets); he has covered your heads (the seers). For you this whole vision is nothing but words sealed in a scroll. And if you give the scroll to someone who can read, and say to him, "Read this, please," he will answer, "I can't; it is sealed."** *Or if you give the scroll to someone who cannot read, and say, "Read this, please," he will answer, "I don't know how to read"* (Isaiah 29:9-12).

In a closed heaven situation, the word of God is rare, dreams are few, and there are not many visions. Also there is a famine of supernatural miracles, wonders, and signs from God. Notice when the heaven is closed over a place, individuals may experience occasional access to the third heaven in response to personal intercession and righteous living.

There are things we do or do not do that can cause the heaven to become inaccessible from the earth. Let us now look at some instances in the Scriptures when the heaven over a place was closed. The people could not receive revelations from God and their word could not reach up to God in heaven because of certain issues.

Closed Heaven Causes

1. Sins and iniquities

   *Surely the arm of the Lord is not too short to save, nor **His ear too dull to hear**. But **your iniquities have separated you from your God**; your sins have hidden His face from you, so that He will not hear* (Isaiah 59:1-2).

2. Not paying attention to what God is saying to us

   If you had responded to My rebuke, I would have poured out My heart to you and made My thoughts known to you. But since you rejected Me when I called and no one gave heed when I stretched out My hand, since you ignored all My advice and would not accept My rebuke, I in turn will laugh at your disaster; I will mock when calamity overtakes you—when calamity overtakes you like a storm, when disaster sweeps over you like a whirlwind, when distress and trouble overwhelm you. ***Then they will call to Me but I will not answer; they will look for Me but will not find me*** *(Proverbs 1:23-28).*

3. To persist in sins and not repent

   "The days are coming," declares the Sovereign Lord, "when I will send a famine through the land—not a famine of food or a thirst for water, but a famine of hearing the words of the Lord. Men will stagger from sea to sea and wander from north to east, searching for the word of the Lord, but they will not find it (Amos 8:11-12).

4. Dishonouring God

   Now a man of God came to Eli and said to him, "This is what the Lord says: 'Did I not clearly reveal Myself to your father's house when they were in Egypt under Pharaoh? I chose your father out of all the tribes of Israel to be My priest, to go up to my altar, to burn incense, and to wear an ephod in My presence. I also gave your father's house all the offerings made with fire by the Israelites. Why do you scorn

My sacrifice and offering that I prescribed for My dwelling? Why do you honour your sons more than Me by fattening yourselves on the choice parts of every offering made by My people Israel?' (1 Samuel 2:27-29)

The boy Samuel ministered before the Lord under Eli. In those days the word of the Lord was rare; there were not many visions (1 Samuel 3:1).

5. Forgetting, not waiting, fleshly desires, testing God

The following points as causes of brass heaven can be deduced from Psalm 106.

*But they **soon forgot what He had done** and **did not wait for His counsel**. In the desert they gave in to their craving; in the wasteland **they put God to the test**. So He gave them what they asked for, but sent a wasting disease upon them (Psalm 106:13-15).*

- Forgetting what God has done in the past.
- Not waiting for His counsel.
- Living according to the desires of the flesh (their craving).
- Putting God to the test.

DISMANTLING A BRASS HEAVEN

Often to dismantle a brass heaven, there is the need for corporate repentance and a crying out together to God. The presence of a brass heaven is temporary, and is definitely not the will of God; we can work at it to allow God to execute His divine justice over the place and establish an open heaven.

The following scriptural examples reveal several ways how dismantling a closed heaven was accomplished corporately in biblical days.

1. Humbling ourselves before God

if My people, who are called by My name, will humble themselves and pray and seek My face and turn from their wicked ways, then will I hear from heaven and will forgive their sin and will heal their land. (2 Chronicles 7:14).

2. Crying out to God

The Israelites did evil in the eyes of the Lord; they forgot the Lord their God and served the Baals and the Asherahs. The anger of the Lord burned against Israel so that He sold them into the hands of Cushan-rishathaim king of Aram Naharaim, to whom the Israelites were subject for eight years. **But when they cried out to the Lord, He raised up for them a deliverer,** *Othniel son of Kenaz, Caleb's younger brother, who saved them* (Judges 3:7-9).

The Lord said, "I have indeed seen the misery of My people in Egypt. **I have heard them crying out because of their slave drivers,** *and I am concerned about their suffering. So I have come down to rescue them from the hand of the Egyptians and to bring them up out of that land into a good and spacious land, a land flowing with milk and honey—the home of the Canaanites, Hittites, Amorites, Perizzites, Hivites and Jebusites.* **And now the cry of the Israelites has reached Me,** *and I have seen the way the Egyptians are oppressing them. So now, go. I am sending you to Pharaoh to bring My people the Israelites out of Egypt." But Moses said to God, "Who am I, that I should go to Pharaoh and bring the Israelites out of Egypt?"* (Exodus 3:7-11)

3. The cry of the innocent people, such as children

When the water in the skin was gone, she put the boy under one of the bushes. Then she went off and sat down nearby, about a bow-shot away, for she thought, "I cannot watch the boy die." And as she sat there nearby, she began to sob. God heard the boy crying, and the angel of God called to Hagar from heaven and said to her, "What is the matter, Hagar? Do not be afraid; God has heard the boy crying as he lies there. Lift the boy up and take him by the hand, for I will make him into a great nation." Then God opened her eyes and she saw a well of water. So she went and filled the skin with water and gave the boy a drink (Genesis 21:15-19).

4. Prayers of other saints in intercession

Another angel, who had a golden censer, came and stood at the altar. He was given much incense to offer, with the prayers of all the saints, on the golden altar before the throne. The smoke of the incense, together with the prayers of the saints, went up before God from the angel's hand. Then the angel took the censer, filled it with fire from the altar, and hurled it on the earth; and there came peals of thunder, rumblings, flashes of lightning and an earthquake (Revelation 8:3-5).

POINTS TO PONDER

1. In a closed heaven situation, the word of God is rare, dreams are few, and there are not many visions. Also there is a famine of supernatural miracles, wonders, and signs from God. You may experience occasional access to the third heaven, though, in response to personal intercession and righteous living. Have you experienced this type of closed heaven situation? Did a commitment to prayer and righteous living make a difference?

2. Of the five causes for a closed heaven, which one keeps you from receiving access to the third heaven the most?

3. Have you been part of a corporate (or personal) dismantling of a closed, or brass, heaven? Remember, or imagine, that circumstance and exactly what God expected of you.

Chapter 12

PICTORIAL VISIONS

M OST PEOPLE RECEIVE pictorial revelations at various times in their lives. However, more commonly pictorial visions are received during prayer sessions. All through the Scriptures it is evident that a prayerful atmosphere creates a ripe environment for manifestation of an open heaven particularly picture revelations. Pictorial, or snapshot, revelations are visions without motion. They are more common than usually appreciated, and are, unfortunately, often discarded even though the Bible is full of instances of God speaking through them. Nowhere is it truer than in the arena of pictorial visions to say that a picture is worth more than a thousand words.

Most pictorial visions are meant to stir up reaction in the recipient to what the Father might be doing in heaven or He may want to communicate. They are snapshot visions that help direct our focus to the essential issue of the time. Because pictorial visions are without motion, there are endless possible meanings to a single picture. To help direct us in the right way, God gives clues. In practice, it seems that God gives hints to the correct meaning of the pictorial revelation immediately following the vision. I have also observed from studying the Scriptures that pictorial visions, snapshot visions, are usually followed by divine clues to help with understanding. Unfortunately, if we do not pay attention to the revelation itself, we are more likely not to notice the divine clues that often follow them.

Some people are more prone to receiving pictorial visions than other forms of visual revelations. A majority of these people are intercessors. Others are prophetic people whose prophetic utterances are often triggered by pictorial (snapshot) visions. There are many other possible reasons why some people are prone to receive snapshot visions including:

- Simply a sovereign choice of God to give them snapshot visions.

- May be due to the uniqueness of the individual's gifting, which makes the person more prone to appreciate pictorial (snapshot) revelation; appears to receive predominantly through pictorial visions.

- Those who are more sensitive and alert in the spirit to pick up visionary revelations of all kinds (including pictorial visions).

- May include a subgroup of people who, although they have the Seer anointing, have not yet developed their gifting to its fullness, hence appear to be more receptive to receiving by pictures only.

Snapshot vision can often be the basis or the starting point of great revelatory encounters in God or even as the signal for the healing power of God that may be available for the time and place. Pictorial visions may also serve as prophecy signals. A prophecy signal is a prompting from God that triggers the prophetic anointing in the person. In general, prophetic signal may be a natural thing or a spiritual occurrence, such as snapshot vision.

Like other forms of visions, pictorial visions are often related to and may be occasioned by the prevailing circumstances in the life of the recipient. For instance, in the Book of Zechariah, the prophet Zechariah had a series of visions (recorded in Zechariah 1:6–6:8) that offered encouragement to the returnees engaged with rebuilding Jerusalem. At the time of Zechariah, the rebuilding program in Jerusalem was under attack from a Persian official (see Ezra 5-6). So this was a crucial time in the history of the Israelites, and these pictorial visions were received at a time when they were waiting to know if Darius the king would allow them to continue the rebuilding project. Zechariah gave his messages based on these visions. The essence of the series of visions was that God would not abandon the Jews to the Persian enemies, but would in the long run show His plan for Israel.

The following compilations are scriptural examples of snapshot visions and how they were immediately followed by a divine clue or interpretation that helped people understand them. I hope by studying them you will gain valuable insight to help you understanding your pictorial revelations.

Pictorial (Snapshot) Vision	Meaning Immediately Following	Points to Note
Golden lampstand		
Zechariah 4:2	Zechariah 4:6	The message of this pictorial vision: as long as Zerubbabel remains connected to the source of his anointing—*the priestly and the kingly aspects of the anointing,* the eyes and the light of the Spirit of God will continue to help him, and he would succeed by the Spirit of God and not by his physical strength.
He asked me, "What do you see?" I answered, "I see a solid gold lampstand with a bowl at the top and seven lights on it, with seven channels to the lights.	*So he said to me, "This is the word of the Lord to Zerubbabel: 'Not by might nor by power, but by my Spirit,' says the Lord Almighty.*	
		The essence is that God will empower His people by the Holy Spirit.
		The lampstand was made of one piece of hammered gold (see Num. 8:4); symbolically indicates that the lampstand anointing comes after molding by God.
		Gold symbolic of durability and divinity;
		bowl as the receptacle for the oil and it is symbolic of the heart of man, and
		oil is symbolic of the anointing.
		The seven lights represent the seven spirits of God "that is seen everywhere around the world."

Pictorial (Snapshot) Vision	Meaning Immediately Following	Points to Note

Two Olive Trees

Zechariah 4:3

Also there are two olive trees by it, one on the right of the bowl and the other on its left.

The Bible gives two interpretations for the meaning of two olive trees:

1. *And a second time I said to him, what are these two olive branches which are besides the two golden tubes or sprouts by which the golden oil is emptied out? And he answered me, Do you not know what these are? And I said, No, my Lord. Then said he, These are the two sons of oil [Joshua, the high priest and Zerubbabel the prince of Judah, the two anointed ones], who stand before the Lord of the whole earth [as His anointed instruments]* (Zech. 4:12-14 AMP).

2. *These [witnesses] are two olive trees and the two lampstands which stands before the Lord of the earth* (Rev. 11:4 AMP).

The two olive trees act as symbols in this pictorial vision, which had immediate relevance to the Jewish returnees in the days of Zerubbabel and a later, futuristic meaning in the Book of Revelation. This is one of the cardinal features of symbolism that is to unfold its meaning in stages: 1. Immediate relevance and 2. Future relevance.

Olive trees generally symbolize a source of anointing; for Zerubbabel its immediate meaning was *the priestly and the kingly aspects of the anointing of God* that would be instruments from God to help him.

The Bible later states that Jesus Christ will rule with both kingly and priestly anointing with perfect harmony:

Tell him (Joshua) that the Lord of Host says, "You represent the Man who will come whose name is "The Branch" — He will grow up from himself — and will build the Temple of the Lord. To Him belongs the royal title. He will rule both as King and as Priest, with perfect harmony between the two.

Symbolically the two olive trees represent the aspect anointing of Jesus Christ to help build the temple.

Pictorial (Snapshot) Vision	Meaning Immediately Following	Points to Note
Almond Tree Branch		
Jeremiah 1:11	Jeremiah 1:12	*An almond tree* draws the farmer's attention to imminent *change in season;* a symbol of wake-up call (a watcher tree).
The word of the Lord came to me:"What do you see, Jeremiah?""I see the branch of an almond tree," I replied.	*The Lord said to me,"You have seen correctly, for I am watching to see that my word is fulfilled."*	A token of an early spring, the harbinger of spring.
		Also marks the beginning of *blooming season.*
		Sign that it is *time for God to fulfill* His promise (early execution of God's will).

Pictorial (Snapshot) Vision	Meaning Immediately Following	Points to Note
Boiling Pot		
Jeremiah 1:13	Jeremiah 1:14-16	In this vision, the *boiling pot* symbolizes:
The word of the Lord came to me again: "What do you see?" "I see a boiling pot, tilting away from the north," I answered.	*The Lord said to me, "From the north disaster will be poured out on all who live in the land. I am about to summon all the peoples of the northern kingdoms," declares the Lord. "Their kings will come and set up their thrones in the entrance of the gates of Jerusalem; they will come against all her surrounding walls and against all the towns of Judah. I will pronounce my judgments on My people because of their wickedness in forsaking Me, in burning incense to other gods and in worshiping what their hands have made."*	• Imminent disaster • God's judgment • Danger from a mightier force • Punishment from God • The principal attack on Judah and Jerusalem would come from the north • Later, in the Book of Jeremiah, the prophet identified the "terror from the north" as Babylon that would come against Israel (see Jer. 20:4).

Pictorial (Snapshot) Vision	Meaning Immediately Following	Points to Note
Swarms of Locust		
Amos 7:1	Amos 7:2-3	*"The king's share"* in this vision connotes:
*This is what the Sovereign Lord showed me: He was preparing swarms of **locusts** after **the king's share** had been harvested and just as the second crop was coming up.*	*When they had stripped the land clean, I cried out, "Sovereign Lord, forgive! How can Jacob survive? He is so small!" So the Lord relented. "This will not happen," the Lord said.*	• The first fruit that belongs to the Lord or the portion taken as tax • The choicest portion (the best portion) • The main portion *Locust* in this context symbolizes • The destroyer of harvest • Impending danger targeted at the harvest • A *wasting process* on the *means of livelihood* • After the king's share indicates the remnant after the king's portion, which is what the people are supposed to survive on and therefore if destroyed represents a crippling economy, with no means of survival.

Pictorial (Snapshot) Vision	Meaning Immediately Following	Points to Note
Plumb Line of Judgment		
Amos 7:7	Amos 7:8-9	*Plum line* in this vision represents God's measuring stick, which has been set in place among the people for generations to come. In this instance it signifies impending judgment.
This is what he showed me: the Lord was standing by a wall that had been built true to plumb, with a plumb line in His hand.	*And the Lord asked me, "What do you see, Amos?" "A plumb line," I replied. Then the Lord said, "Look, I am setting a plumb line among My people Israel; I will spare them no longer. The high places of Isaac will be destroyed and the sanctuaries of Israel will be ruined; with My sword I will rise against the house of Jeroboam."*	

- Israel's time of grace has run out, and God is set to bring the work of everyone to test; those found wanting shall not be spared any longer.
- The high places represent the places of idolatry and the corrupt temple.
- God's judgment against sin in the land of Israel.
- The sins reminiscent of the sins of Jeroboam kingship.
- The house of Jeroboam mentioned here could possibly refer to the corrupt dynasty of Jeroboam; both Jeroboam I and Jeroboam II (Jeroboam II was reigning at the time Amos gave this prophecy).
- Though God is the God of mercy, He will, however, not negotiate the need and importance for us to have right standing before Him.
- See also 2 Kings 21:13.

Pictorial (Snapshot) Vision	Meaning Immediately Following	Points to Note
Plum Line of Blessing		
Zechariah 2:1-2	Zechariah 2:3-5	*This measuring stick (plumb line) indicates the need to* ascertain that the foundation is strong enough to hold the expected blessings.
Then I looked up—and there before me was a man with a measuring line in his hand! I asked,"Where are you going?"He answered me,"To measure Jerusalem, to find out how wide and how long it is."	*Then the angel who was speaking to me left, and another angel came to meet him and said to him:"Run, tell that young man, 'Jerusalem will be a city without walls because of the great number of men and livestock in it. And I myself will be a wall of fire around it,' declares the Lord, 'and I will be its glory within.'*	Technically, a plum line is a string with a weight tied to the end to establish a vertical line and ensure a straight line to build a straight wall. The meaning of this vision:
		• The *city* will be restored.
	The purpose of this plumb line is for rebuilding Jerusalem.	• *Jerusalem* will be a city without walls overflowing with people and livestock.
		• *Also a picture of the future Church of Christ.*
Basket of Ripe Fruit		
Amos 8:2a	Amos 8:2b	In this vision, *a basket* represents:
"What do you see, Amos?"he asked."A basket of ripe fruit,"I answered.	*Then the Lord said to me,"The time is ripe for my people Israel; I will spare them no longer.*	• A measure of something
		• A measure of time
		The *ripe fruit* symbolizes in the context of this vision:
		• The appointed time
		• The right time
		• Readiness
		• That which can not be delayed any longer

Pictorial (Snapshot) Vision	Meaning Immediately Following	Points to Note
Basket of Ripe Figs		
Jeremiah 24:1-2	Jeremiah 24:4-7	In this vision, the basket of ripe figs was a symbol of quality and goodness.
After Jehoiachin son of Jehoiakim king of Judah and the officials, the craftsmen and the artisans of Judah were carried into exile from Jerusalem to Babylon by Nebuchadnezzar king of Babylon, the Lord showed me two baskets of figs placed in front of the temple of the Lord. One basket had very good figs, like those that ripen early; the other basket had very poor figs, so bad that they could not be eaten.	*Then the word of the Lord came to me: "This is what the Lord, the God of Israel, says: 'Like these good figs, I regard as good the exiles from Judah, whom I sent away from this place to the land of the Babylonians. My eyes will watch over them for their good, and I will bring them back to this land. I will build them up and not tear them down; I will plant them and not uproot them. I will give them a heart to know Me, that I am the Lord. They will be My people, and I will be their God, for they will return to Me with all their heart.*	Notice that the ripeness here connotes goodness and not a measure of readiness. (Ripeness of fruits indicated readiness in prophet Amos' vision of the basket of ripe fruits.) Therefore ripeness could mean different things depending on the context of the vision or dream.

The good figs are symbolic of the deported exiles, God has set them apart for Himself; God would bring them back. God would give them a new heart that would know Him and the new covenant (see Jer. 31:31-34). |

Pictorial (Snapshot) Vision	Meaning Immediately Following	Points to Note
Basket of Ripe Figs continued.		
	Jeremiah 24:8-10 *"'But like the poor figs, which are so bad that they cannot be eaten,' says the Lord, 'so will I deal with Zedekiah king of Judah, his officials and the survivors from Jerusalem, whether they remain in this land or live in Egypt. I will make them abhorrent and an offence to all the kingdoms of the earth, a reproach and a byword, an object of ridicule and cursing, wherever I banish them. I will send the sword, famine and plague against them until they are destroyed from the land I gave to them and their fathers.'"*	*The bad figs* represent the depraved moral and spiritual state of the people who remained in Jerusalem after the deportation of exiles to Babylon. They were those who would flee to Egypt and face trouble, shame, and calamity. They would become unusable to God.

Pictorial (Snapshot) Vision	Meaning Immediately Following	Points to Note
Inescapable Judgment of God		Pictorial Vision with Phrases
Amos 9:1	Amos 9:2-4	The *symbolic action and the accompanying phrases* indicate:
I saw the Lord standing by the altar, and He said:"Strike the tops of the pillars so that the thresholds shake. Bring them down on the heads of all the people; those who are left I will kill with the sword. Not one will get away, none will escape.	*Though they dig down to the depths of the grave, from there My hand will take them. Though they climb up to the heavens, from there I will bring them down. Though they hide themselves on the top of Carmel, there I will hunt them down and seize them. Though they hide from me at the bottom of the sea, there I will command the serpent to bite them. Though they are driven into exile by their enemies, there I will command the sword to slay them. I will fix My eyes upon them for evil and not for good.*	• That the long arm of God and His judgment is inescapable for those who refused to repent. • No one can hide from God. • God can use the evil one as an instrument of judgment. • No foundation or pillar can protect one if God decrees judgment. • God would start at the altar to destroy the sinful nations of Israel. • Top of Carmel represents the highest point on the earth at the time. • The bottom of the sea represents the lowest point of the earth. Both representing the fact that no one can hide from God.

Pictorial (Snapshot) Vision	Meaning Immediately Following	Points to Note
Watchful Eyes of the Lord		
Zechariah 1:8	Zechariah 1:9-10	In this encounter:
During the night I had a vision—and there before me was a man riding a red horse! He was standing among the myrtle trees in a ravine. Behind him were red, brown and white horses.	*I asked, "What are these, my lord?" The angel who was talking with me answered, "I will show you what they are." Then the man standing among the myrtle trees explained, "They are the ones the Lord has sent to go throughout the earth."* This is the vision of the watchfulness of God over Israel—a message of hope for the Jews who have returned from Babylonian captivity.	• The *horse* represents powerful spiritual messengers sent by God to the earth. • There is no consensus on what the colors symbolize. Some think that the color stands for the geographical area assigned to the messenger as well as the nature of the power or the method of operation of the messenger. Within the context of this vision: • *Red* signifies war and bloodshed • *Brown* indicates hunger, famine, or pestilence. • *White* represents the time for complete prosperity and God's righteousness. • *The Angel of the Lord* was also riding on a red horse. Here *red* indicates the *blood of Jesus* and signifies warning.

Pictorial (Snapshot) Vision	Meaning Immediately Following	Points to Note
Four Horns		
Zechariah 1:18	Zechariah 1:19	In the context of this vision:
Then I looked up—and there before me were four horns!	*I asked the angel who was speaking to me, "What are these?" He answered me, "These are the horns that scattered Judah, Israel and Jerusalem."*	• *A horn* is a symbol of power and authority—and in this case, hostility. • *The four horns* represent the powerful four kingdoms that scattered the Jewish people before Zechariah's time, *Assyria, Egypt, Babylon, and Medo-Persia.*

Pictorial (Snapshot) Vision	Meaning Immediately Following	Points to Note
Four Craftsmen		
Zechariah 1:20 *Then the Lord showed me four craftsmen.*	Zechariah 1:21 *I asked, "What are these coming to do?" He answered, "These are the horns that scattered Judah so that no one could raise his head, but the craftsmen have come to terrify them and throw down these horns of the nations who lifted up their horns against the land of Judah to scatter its people."* **God's Fourscore Acts of Judgment** *For thus says the Lord God: How much more, when I send my fourscore acts of judgments upon Jerusalem, the Sword, the famine, the evil wild beasts and the pestilence—to cut off from it man and beast"(Ezek. 14:21).*	• The *four craftsmen* are the more powerful instrument of judgment that God has raised against the evil four horns. • According to *Ezekiel 14:21*, these four craftmen were symbolic of the *sword, famine, wild beasts, and plagues.* • God is able to raise equal or even greater force against any onslaught the enemy can muster against us.

Pictorial (Snapshot) Vision	Meaning Immediately Following	Points to Note
Flying Scroll		
Zechariah 5:2	Zechariah 5:3	*A scroll* is a rolled parchment, an ancient equivalent of a book. The scroll was unfolded in the vision indicating that the word will reveal or be exposed in such a way that all can read it.
He asked me, "What do you see?" I answered, "I see a flying scroll, thirty feet long and fifteen feet wide."	*And he said to me, "This is the curse that is going out over the whole land; for according to what it says on one side, every thief will be banished, and according to what it says on the other, everyone who swears falsely will be banished."*	• The word or the laws of God has no limitation and its jurisdiction has no restriction. • It is capable of bringing judgment to those who steal and to those who swear falsely. • The curse is the judgment spoken and contained in the scroll; the scroll contained the judgment of God on those who steal or tell lies by the name of God! "They have been judged and sentenced to death." Sadly, this particular curse was irrevocable.

Pictorial (Snapshot) Vision	Meaning Immediately Following	Points to Note
Measuring Basket		
Zechariah 5:6a	Zechariah 5:6b	The wickedness of the people is measured and taken away to a place of iniquities ready for judgment on a later date.
I asked, "What is it?" He replied, "It is a measuring basket."	*And he added, "This is the iniquity of the people throughout the land."*	
		The woman is symbolic of wickedness that was taken and then consigned, just as she was pushed back to confinement.
		The mystery of the two women with winds in their wings is uncertain, but they appear as probable agents of God.

As these pictorial visions have important meaning and consequences for those who receive them, likewise the interpretations of dreams and visions are crucial for maturing into His glory for us. The next chapter sums up the difference between dream interpretation (see Chapter 6) and vision interpretation.

POINTS TO PONDER

1. Most pictorial visions are meant to stir up reaction in you to what the Father might be doing in heaven or He may want to communicate. These are snapshot visions that help direct your focus to the essential issue of the time. Because pictorial visions are without motion, there are endless possible meanings to a single picture. Have pictorial visions impacted your life?

    _____

    _____

2. Pictorial visions, or snapshot visions, are usually followed by divine clues to help you understand. If you don't pay attention to the revelation itself, you are more likely not to notice the divine clues that often follow them. How good are you at seeking clues for the meaning of revelation?

    _____

    _____

3. Snapshot vision can often be the basis or the starting point of great revelatory encounters in God or even as the signal for the healing power of God that may be available for the time and place. Pictorial visions may also serve as prophecy signals. Has a snapshot vision opened your spiritual awareness for more of what God destined for you?

    _____

    _____

Chapter 13

VISION VERSUS DREAM INTERPRETATION

IN THE RECEPTION OF *visions*, there is varying degree of mind alertness and differing points of involvement of the natural realm. This is not so with *dreams*. In dreams, usually the mind does not participate in direct reception of dreams. As the mind could directly participate in the reception of visions, visions are therefore more likely to impact the mind of the recipient during the visionary reception with valuable insights that could help with the understanding of the vision. Unlike dreams, most visions, even those with complex symbolism, leave the recipient with divine prompting as to their meaning. Mind alertness makes the mind more receptive to God's prompting through word of knowledge that may be available during the visionary reception.

Most people in established prophetic ministries experience many revelatory visual signal or snapshot visions with very significant mind alertness. The result is that most of these prophetic people, therefore, come out of these experiences with remarkable insight about the meaning of the visionary encounters. The downside to this is that there is a tendency for these prophetic people to expect other dreamers to come out of their dream experiences with a similar degree of insightful impartation. But this does not generally occur in dream encounters, as the mind is usually asleep during dream reception. Therefore mind alertness during the reception of visions makes the interpretation of vision slightly different from the interpretation of dreams.

Also, mind alertness makes it easier for interaction with God in visionary encounters, such as exemplified by the common interactive exchanges in trances. For instance, in Acts 10:14, apostle Peter had a vision in which he was able to interact with God because he retained appropriate awareness of his true natural identity and consciousness during the encounter. He says, *"Surely not, Lord" Peter replied. "I have never eaten anything impure or unclean."* For appropriate interaction with God during the spiritual encounter, one has to be able to carry into or able to retain an appreciable degree of consciousness or awareness of one's true natural situation during the encounter. Mind alertness makes this more readily attainable in visions.

VISION INTERPRETATION SUMMARY

- Visions can be received when the eyes, mind, and other natural senses are awake and alert.

- Interactive communication with God is easily attainable in vision or visionary encounters because of varying degrees of mind alertness.

- The human mind is variably involved in the reception and therefore processing of visions.

- During reception of visions, divine word of knowledge impartation can take place so that understanding is planted in the mind of the recipient.

- For most people, visions are literal and appear to be more real than dreams.

- Because of the combination of these factors, visions are often easier to understand.

- From my experience, symbolism is remarkably minimized in most visions. However, there are visions with high levels of symbolism.

- In symbolic visions, the understanding of the true meaning of the symbols and symbolic actions are basically the same as in dreams, except when understanding is facilitated by a word of knowledge sown by God at the time of the reception of the vision.

- Exposition or correlation of the relevance of the symbols and actions in the vision to the actual life circumstance is also remarkably influenced by the unique impartation that might have occurred during the visionary encounters.

- The varying degrees of bodily involvement in visions provide a framework for healing or even physical harm. Physical tiredness or even physical harm can therefore occur readily in visions.

- Visions carry a greater degree of being able to impact the body and the soul of the recipient than dreams. But on the other hand, dreams are more able to connect the dreamer with God's heart.

Visions may therefore be more easily interpreted but would require *careful evaluation, proclamation, and application.* Reception and understanding visions are less susceptible to hindrances emanating from the personal situation of the recipient—lack of peace, pressures of life, or evil revelatory delays—than in dreams, because of the direct mind participation in the reception of visions and the subsequent easy understanding that often follows. In seasons of low dream reception, God is often able to speak to the person with visionary messages. Above all, as with the interpretation of dreams, only by the Holy Spirit can one gain understanding of visions.

POINTS TO PONDER

1. Mind alertness makes it easier for interaction with God in visionary encounters, such as exemplified by the common interactive exchanges in trances. Apostle Peter had a vision in which he was able to interact with God because he retained appropriate awareness of his true natural identity and consciousness during the encounter. How alert is your mind? Is it prepared to accept what God desires to offer you?

2. For appropriate interaction with God during a spiritual encounter, you have to be able to carry into or retain an appreciable degree of consciousness or awareness of your true natural situation. Are you ready, willing, and able?

3. Visions may be more easily interpreted but require *careful evaluation, proclamation, and application.* In seasons of low dream reception, God is often able to speak to you with visionary messages. As with the interpretation of dreams, only by the Holy Spirit can you gain understanding of vision. Do you seek the Holy Spirit's guidance first?

Chapter 14

CONCLUSION

YOU ARE NOW well aware of how God used dreams and visions at critical points to guide and direct the lives of people and nations in biblical days.
Through the numerous Old and New Testament Scriptures cited for you, you realize that dreams carried special significance then—and are often one of the ways God
still uses to make known His will to us.

Concerning the present age, God also says, *"If there is a prophet among you, I,
the Lord, make Myself known to him in a vision; I speak to him in a dream"* (Num.
12:6).

And speaking of the future, God says, *"It shall come to pass in the last days, says
God, that I will pour out of My Spirit on all flesh; your sons and daughters shall prophesy, your young men shall see visions and your old men shall dream dreams"* (Acts
2:17).

God continues to speak to us through dreams and visions and will speak through
them in the future. We can no longer afford to be silent about dreams and visions.
Everyone dreams. Everyone wonders if their dreams mean anything. It is time to
acknowledge their existence and do something to bring the light of God into the
situation. We cannot continue to sit back and allow innocent people to drift into
darkness and into the hands of the prince of the darkness.

As mentioned in the Introduction, the more the church distances itself from
this valuable means of divine communication, the more erroneous and frustrating interpretation drives honest Christians into spiritual bondage. The rapidly

expanding occult culture is distributing literature and misinformation about dreams and visions that many consider true when in reality it is full of deception, profiteering, and confusion on this subject.

Modern-day lies about dreams and superstitious attitudes regarding visions are because dreams and visions happen to Christians and non-Christians alike. Without the Holy Spirit, the majority of non-believers treat dreams and visions as omens and seek to utilize them outside God's plans and purposes. Such practices amount to using godly principles in an ungodly way and are a form of divination. Consequently, the image of dreams and visions within the Christian community has been tainted. Let us carefully restore this valuable means of divine communication using biblical methods.

After all, our greatest asset on earth is not only our ability to hear from God, but also our ability to both hear and understand what God is saying to us. Dreams and visions are sure ways for God to direct believers' steps and will remain exciting and revealing ways to bring the agenda of Heaven to earth.

PART III

CONDENSED DICTIONARY
OF DREAM SYMBOLS

ACID: Something that eats from within. Keeping offense or hatred or malice.

Symbolic Actions

1. *Seeing acid in a container:* Potentially dangerous situation, something to be handled with care.

2. *Acid smeared on the skin:* Challenging situation, something that could be dangerous and corrosive.

See to it that no one misses the grace of God and that no bitter root grows up to cause trouble and defile many (Hebrews 12:15).

ADULTERY: Unfaithfulness regarding things of the spirit or of the natural, or actual adultery; lust for the pleasures of this world; sin.

Symbolic Actions

1. *When a married person dreams of having extra-marital affairs:* May indicate dreamer unfaithful in things of God, or may be literal or tempting situation, divided loyalty, wavering between options.

2. *When a married man dreams of looking for a person to marry:* May indicate the need to fully identify one's calling in God; the dreamer is not completely settled into the marriage relation; the need to be more intimate with one's spouse.

3. *When the dreamer suspects spouse is in extra-marital affair:* This may commonly indicate that one's spouse is paying too much attention to things like business or profession. From my experience, however, this may only occasionally be literal.

The acts of the sinful nature are obvious: sexual immorality, impurity and debauchery; idolatry and witchcraft; hatred, discord, jealousy, fits of rage, selfish ambition, dissensions, factions (Galatians 5:19-20).

You adulterous people, don't you know that friendship with the world is hatred toward God? Anyone who chooses to be a friend of the world becomes an enemy of God (James 4:4).

AIRPLANE: A personal ministry or a church; capable of moving in the Holy Spirit. Flowing in high spiritual power. Holy spirit-powered ministry.

Symbolic Actions

1. *Crashing:* The end of one phase or change of direction.

2. *High Flying:* Fully-powered in the Spirit.

3. *Low Flying:* Only partially operative in the Spirit.

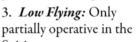

4. *Aircraft Soaring:* Deep in the Spirit or moving in the deep things of God.

5. *Warplane:* Call to intercessory ministry; things of present or spiritual warfare.

NOTE: **ACID — AIRPPLANE**
are excerpts from
Bible-Based Dictionary of Prophetic Symbols for Every Christian by Dr. Joe Ibojie

Airport: This often refers to the ministry that sends out missionaries; high-powered spiritual church capable of equipping and sending out ministries;

ministry in preparation or capable of providing or nourishing others in readiness for service.

Alligator: a large-mouthed enemy; verbal attacks.

Altar: a place set apart for spiritual rituals or prayers/worship, whether good or bad.

Anchor: the pillar that an object or person hangs on, or builds hope upon.

Ankles: little faith; early stages.

Anoint: equipping with the Holy Spirit for service; the power of Holy Spirit to do a work; sanctification to be set apart.

Ant: industrious; ability to plan ahead; conscious of seasons of life; unwanted guest.

Ark: an object of strength; relating to God's presence.

Arm: power and strength, whether good or bad.

Armies: spiritual warriors, whether good or bad.

Arrows: powerful words, whether good or bad; Word of God; curses from the devil; spiritual children; good or bad intentions.

Ashes: signs of repentance or sorrow.

Attic: the mind zone; a thought process; the spirit realm; memories/past issues/stored up materials.

Autograph: prominence or fame.

Autumn: transition; end of one phase and beginning of another.

Axe: the Word of God; to encourage by kind words; issues that needs to be settled.

Baby: new Christians; the beginning of something new; beginning to be productive; something in its infancy or early stages.

Back: pertaining to the past; something behind, concealed, or hidden; out of view.

Backside: something in the past or behind the dreamer; something concealed from view or understanding.

Baking: making provision for feeding people; preparation for welfare ministry; God's provision.

Balances: something reflecting both sides of the matter; waiting to tilt, one way or the other; judgment.

Balm: healing; anointing; something to relieve pains, stress, or agony.

Bank: heavenly account; God's favor for a future season; a place of safety and security; God's provision.

Banner (or flag): the covering to which everyone belongs or is committed to; something that brings unity, love, or purpose; a unifying object or circumstance; victory.

Banquet: God's provision; a full cup; plentiful affluence and abundance; satisfaction; blessing; celebration; structured teaching of the Word of God.

Bareness: unproductive; a difficult time or period.

Barn: a place of provision; a church; stored spiritual wealth.

Basement: the unseen part of something; storage zone; related to the foundation; hidden.

Basket: a measure of God's provision; a measure of judgment.

Bathroom: a period of cleansing/entering a time of repentance; a place of voluntary nakedness or facing reality in individual life.

Beam: power or illumination coming from God or the heavenly; a time of exposure or spotlight.

Bear: danger; wicked person or spirit; vindictiveness; evil; something that is after what you possess.

Bedroom: a place of intimacy; a place of rest, sleep, or dreams; a place of covenant; a place of revelation.

Bees: more noisy than effective; a double-edged situation capable of going bad; producing sweetness.

Bells: call to attention or action; to bring to alertness; to say it loudly; public warning.

Belly: feelings; desires; spiritual well-being; sentiment.

Bicycle: a ministry depending on much human effort; a one-man ministry.

Binoculars: looking ahead; looking into the future; prophetic ministry.

Bird: symbol of leader, whether evil or good at different levels; Holy Spirit or evil spirit.

Black: lack; famine; evil; demonic spirit; darkness.

Bleeding: hurting; losing spirituality; verbal accusation; traumatic.

Blind: lack of understanding; ignorance; not able to see into the Spirit world.

Blood: atonement; to appease; something that testifies.

Blood Transfusion: getting new life; rescuing situation.

Blue: spiritual; Heaven-related visitation from God or the Holy Spirit.

Boat: a ministry capable of influencing many people.

Body Odor: unclean spirit; after-effect of fleshy actions.

Bones: the substance of something; the main issue; long lasting; (if a skeleton) something without flesh/substance, or details.

Book: gaining understanding/knowledge; Scriptures; revelation; promise from God; message from title of the book.

Bottle: relating to the body as the container of anointing.

Bow: source from which attacks come; (if an arrow) the power of a nation or person; verbal attacks; the tongue.

Bowl: a measure of something.

Bracelet: pertaining to pride; valuable, but of the world; identity, if it has a name.

Breast: source of milk for new Christians; source of sustenance; an object of enticement.

Breastplate: God's protective shield; protective of vital issues.

Bride: the Church's relationship to Jesus; special to Jesus; covenant or relationship.

Bridge: something that takes you across an obstacle, such as faith; a connection between two objects or circumstances; something that holds you up in times of difficulty.

Bridle: put control over, such as self-control over using the tongue; something imposed by a higher authority to effect control, for either good or bad.

Brook: provision of God; something that brings refreshment; wisdom; prosperity from God; if dirty, it means corrupted or contaminated.

Broom: in the process of getting rid of sins; a symbol of witchcraft.

Brother: a Christian brother or sister (spiritual brother); your own brother, or someone with similar qualities.

Building: symbolic of spiritual and emotional being of a place, person, or church; life of a person, church, or office.

Butter: encouragement; something that brings soothing, smooth words.

Cake: provision from Heaven.

Candle: Word of God.

Lamp or electricity: Word of God; symbolic of man's spirit; a lack of God's presence when unlit; conscience.

Candlestick: people who carry the light of God; the lamp stand; Spirit of God; the Church.

Carpenter: Jesus; someone who makes or amends things.

Cat: a deceptive situation/person; unclean spirit; craftiness; witchcraft waiting to attack; a precious habit that could be dangerous; a personal pet.

Cave: safe hiding place; a secret place of encountering God.

Chain: symbolic of bondage or captivity; to be bound in the spirit or in the natural.

Chair: authority over something; coming to position of authority; throne of God.

Cheetah: unclean spirit.

Chicken: an evangelist; gifting; caring spirit; gathering.

Circle (ring or round): a circumstance that is endless and which signifies agreement or covenant; hunting, if making a circle; relating to the universe.

Circumcision: cutting off fleshly things; coming to liberty; covenanting with God; blood relationship; new levels of spiritual walk; born again.

City: the makeup of a person; all that has been input in a person or people; group; church.

B
C

Classroom: a time of spiritual preparation; a person with a gifting to teach others.

Clay: delicate and fragile; not secure; something that refers to frailty of man.

Clock: timing is important in the situation; time to do something revealed; an actual time may refer to Bible passages; running out of time.

Closet: hidden, confidential, personal, or exclusive; a place of prayer.

Clothing: covering, whether pure or impure; your standing or authority in a situation.

Tearing clothes: covering; God is providing; grief and sorrow.

Clouds: heavenly manifestation; glory of God's presence; a dark time of travel; fear, trouble, or storms of life.

Dark clouds: a time of storm.

White clouds: glory of God.

Clown: not a serious person; not taking God seriously; childish.

Coat: mantle; protective covering; righteousness (if clean); not righteous or unclean (if dirty).

College: promotion in the Spirit.

Columns: a spirit of control and manipulation.

Cord: enhancing unity/love; something that holds things together, such as a three-fold cord.

Couch: rest and relaxation; peace.

Countryside: a time of peace/tranquillity; a potential that is not yet explored.

Courthouse: a time of being judged or persecution; trial.

Cow: food/source of enrichment; a potential source of sin.

Crawling: humility or to be humiliated.

Crooked: distorted; not straight.

Crossing Street: changing perspective.

Crown: symbol of authority; seal of power; Jesus Christ; to reign; to be honored.

Crying: actual crying; a period of grief; outburst of sadness; intense emotional expression.

Cultural clothes: call to a nation.

Cup: your portion in life; provision.

Cymbals: an actual object; praise God; without genuine love.

Dam: the power of unity or gathering resources; obstacle to a flow; reserve sustenance; stillness.

Darkness: lack of light.

Daytime: the opportune time; a time of light; a season of good deeds; a season when matters are revealed or understanding is gained.

Deaf: not spiritually attentive; not paying attention.

Death: some measure of dying to self in an area; separation from things of evil; actual physical death.

Deer: Psalm 42; spiritual longing; symbolizes hunger for the things of God; ability to take great strides.

Den: busy doing the wrong activities.

Desert: lack; training; or testing; a place reliant on God.

Diamond: an object to engrave with; a hard object; an object sharp at cutting.

Difficult walking: difficult times of life; facing opposition.

Dining room: feeding on the Word of God; a place of spiritual food; table of the Lord.

Dinosaur: something in the distant past; something big and terrible, but that God has dealt with.

Dirty cloth: false doctrine.

Dirty/Dry: impure spiritual things.

Dirty/Neglected: a place in need of attention.

Disease: emotional upset; bondage from the devil.

Ditch: deception; a trap; fleshy desire; to follow into problems; preparation.

Dog: a pet sin; a gift that could be harnessed to do good, but should not be trusted too much; something that could be versatile in function but unpredictable.

Donkey: an enduring spirit; that which God could use, if surrendered to Him.

Door: an opening; Jesus Christ; the way; a possibility; grace.

Down: spiritual descent or backsliding; falling away; humiliation; failure.

Dragon: satan; high demonic spirit; great level of wickedness; anti-Christ.

Drawing: conceptualization.
Artist's paint: a means or method of illustration; to be fluent in expression.
Paint: doctrine, truth, or deception.

Driver: the one in command or control; the one who makes decisions.

Driving in reverse: not going in a correct direction with anointing.

Drought: a period of lack; without God.

Drowning: overcome by a situation leading to depression; overwhelmed to the point of self-pity.

Drugs: medication; illicit drugs equals counterfeit anointing.

Drunkard: influenced by counterfeit source of anointing; self-indulgence error; uncontrolled lust.

Dust: temporary nature of humanity; frailty of man; curse.

Dynamite: great spiritual power, whether good or bad; Holy Spirit "dynamos."

Ear: symbolic of the prophet, not the seer; hearing spiritual things that either build up or tear down; lack of hearing, or a need to pay more attention.

Eating: feeding on something, such as the Word of God or evil; meditation and gaining greater understanding.

D
E

Egg: delicate seed or promise; sustenance; the possibility for growth, potential, and development in any manner; revelation.

Egypt: bondage or slavery; refuge; old sin; pre-Christian life.

Electricity: spiritual power of God; potential for God; flow.

Electrical outlet: possibility of being connected into the Holy Spirit's flow.

Unplugged cord: not connected to the Spirit's power.

Elementary: the infant stage, not yet mature.

Elevator: moving up and down in levels of godly authority.

Employee/Servants: one who is submitted to authority; the actual person.

Employer/Master: Jesus; the authority, whether good or bad; pastor; evil leadership.

Explosion: quick outburst, generally positive; sudden expansion or increase; quick work or devastating change.

Eyes: seer anointing.

Closed eyes: ignorance; spiritually blindness, mostly self-imposed.

Winking eyes: concealed intention; cunning person.

Factory: structured service in God's vineyard.

Fan: stirring up of gifting; something that brings relief or comfort; makes fire hotter; increasing air circulation.

Farmer: one who plants, nurtures, cares for new Christians; pastor capable of sowing and reaping harvest; Jesus Christ.

Father: Father God; supplier of needs; natural father of the bloodline; one who provides; the head of home or place.

Feathers: protective spiritual covering; weightless; something with which to move into the spiritual realm; the presence of God.

Feeding: to partake in a spiritual provision, good or evil.

Fence: protection; security; self-imposed; limitation; stronghold.

Field: life situation; things to do and accomplish, all depends on the field and context.

Finger: means of discernment; spiritual sensitivity; feelings.

Clenched finger: pride.

Finger of God: work of God, authority of God.

Index finger: prophet.

Middle finger: evangelist.

Pointed finger: accusations, persecution, instructions, direction.

Small finger: pastor.

Thumb: apostle.

Fire: God's presence; trial; persecution; burning fervency; emotion; longing, aching, and craving; power; Holy Spirit; anger, judgment, and punishment.

Fish: new converts to the Lord; newly recreated spirit of man; miraculous provision of food.

Five: grace related to the five-fold ministry.

Flash: revelation or insight.

Flood: judgment on those who use power to inflict violence on others; sin judged; overcome; to be overcome and unable to recover.

Flowers: man's glory of the flesh that is passing away; an offering; glory of God; beautiful expression of love; renewal; Spring; Jesus (if a Lily of the Valley); love, courtship, and romance (if a rose).

Fly: evil spirits; evil corruption; to possess by evil spirit; results of unclean actions.

Flying: highly powered by the Holy Spirit.

Fog: not clear; uncertainty; concealed; vagueness.

Food: spiritual and physical nourishment, either good or evil.

Foreigner: a person outside the Christian faith (not a citizen of Heaven); someone to be taught, cared for, and brought into the covenant.

Forehead: thought process and reasoning; revelation; retaining and recalling ability; commitment to God.

Forest: growth in life, as depending on the context; place of danger and darkness where one can be easily lost and harmed; confusion and lack of direction; uncultivated; undeveloped potentials.

Forty: testing period; season of trial.

Four: worldly creation; four corners of the world; four minds; four seasons; global implication of the four Gospels.

Fourteen: double anointing; recreation; reproduction; Passover.

Fox: a cunning spirit; craftiness, secretly or counter-productive.

Freezer: storing spiritual food for future time.

Friend: brother or sister in Christ, or showing to have similar qualities; faithful person; yourself.

Frog: an evil spirit; noisy; boastful; sorcery; lying nature; issuing curses.

Front side: looking ahead, something in the future.

Furnace: source of heat; the heart; heated and painful experiences; a period of trial.

Garage: symbolic of storage; potential or protection.

Garbage: abandoned things; corruption; reprobate; unclean spirit; departure from all that is godly; something that is thrown away; opinion of life without Jesus.

Garden: field of labor in life; a place of increase, fruitfulness, and productivity; a place of rest or romance.

Gardening: an area of labor; a place of reward, increase, or harvest.

Gasoline: source of energy; faith-filled prayer; danger; sinful motives.

Gate: doors; opening; salvation.

F
G

Giant: a powerful spiritual being, such as an angel or demon; a challenging situation that needs to be overcome.

Girdle: to prepare for use; might potency; to strengthen for readiness; gathering together of the strength within you.

Gloves: something that fits; protects the means of service or productivity.

Goat: pertaining to foolishness; carnal; fleshly; not submitting to authority; walking into sin; need for repentance; miscarriage of judgment, such as scapegoat.

Gold: of God; seal of divinity; God's glory; faithful; endurance; holiness that endures; a symbol of honor; of high valor; a valuable that endures.

Governor: the person who has power in a place; spiritual leader in the church; leader of a geographical region; evil principality; authority; rulership; reigning.

Grandchild: blessing or spirit passed on from previous generation; generational inheritance, either good or bad; heir; spiritual offspring of your ministry.

Grandmother: generational authority over a person; spiritual inheritance; past wisdom or gifting.

Grapes: God's word in seed form; Word of God; fruit of the Promised Land.

Grass: life; something meant to be maintained

Dried grass: death of the flesh through repentance.

Mowed grass: disciplined obedience.

Grasshopper (Locust): a devastating situation; an instrument of God's judgment; low self-esteem.

Graveyard/Grave: old tradition; cultural reserve; death; demonic influence from the past; buried potential.

Grey: uncertainty; compromise; consisting of good and bad mixture.

Green: provision; rest and peace; good or evil life.

Groom: Christ; marriage; headship.

Guard: ability to keep on the right path; spirit of protection; to be vigilant.

Guest: spiritual messenger; an angel or evil presence.

Gun: instrument of demonic affliction; spoken words that wound; power of words in prayer; dominion through speaking the Word of God.

Hail: judgment against God's enemies.

Hair: cover; something numerous; man's glory.

Baldness: grief and shame or lack of wisdom.

Haircut: getting something in correct shape; cutting off a good or evil habit or tradition.

Long hair (maintained): covenant and strength.

Long hair (man): rebellious behavior; covenant relationship.

Long hair (woman): glory on the woman; church submission; wife.

Long unkempt hair: out of control.

Losing hair: loss of wisdom, glory.

Shaving: getting rid of what hinders or is dirty.

Short hair (woman): manliness; not submitting.

To shape: to acquire wisdom.

Hammer: living Word; preaching the Word hard and fast; capable of breaking something to pieces.

Hands: means of service or expressing strength.

Clapping: joy and worship.

Fist: pride in one's strength; anger.

Hands covering face: guilt or shame.

Holding hands: in agreement.

Left hand: something spiritual.

Raised hands: surrender or worshiping.

Right hand: oath of allegiance; means of power and honor; natural strengths.

Shaking hands: coming to an agreement.

Stretched out hands: surrender.

Trembling: to fear; spirit of fear; anxiety; awe at God's presence.

Under thighs: in oaths.

Washing: declaring innocence; to dissociate oneself.

Harlot (or Prostitute): a tempting situation; something that appeals to your flesh; worldly desire; pre-Christian habit that wants to be resurrected; enticement.

Harp: if used for God, praise and worship in Heaven and in the earth; an instrument for praise and worship.

Harvest: seasons of grace; opportunities to share the gospel; fruitfulness; reward of labor and action.

Hat: covering; protection; mantle; crown; protection of the head.

Head: lordship; authority; Jesus/God; husband; master/boss; pastor; mind; thoughts.

Anointed head: set apart for God's service.

Hand-covering head: signifying sorrow.

Hedge: God's safeguard; security; safety.

Heel: a crushing power.

Helicopter: Spirit-powered for spiritual warfare; a one-man ministry.

Helmet: an awareness and inner assurance of salvation; God's promise.

High School: moving into a higher level of walk with God; capable of moving others into a higher walk with God.

Highway: holy way; the path of life; truth of God; Christ; predetermined path of life, or path of life that enjoys high volume usage; may lead to good or evil destinations.

Dead end: a course of action that will lead to nothing.

Gravel road: way; God's Word; stony ground.

Muddy road: difficult path; not clear; uncertain path.

Road with construction: in preparation, change.

H

Hills: a place of exaltation; uplifted high above the natural; the throne of God; Mount Zion.

Hips: reproduction, or relating to reproduction; supporting structure.

Honey: sweet; strength; wisdom; Spirit of God; an abiding anointing; the sweet Word of our Lord.

Horns: the source of anointed power; the power of kings.

Horse: of great strength; powerful in warfare; a spirit of tenacity, not double-minded; a ministry powerful and capable of competing; strength under control, such as meekness. God is judgment.

Bay (flame-colored) horse: power; fire.

Black horse: lack.

Pale horse: spirit of death.

Red horse: danger; passion; the Blood of Jesus.

White horse: purity and righteousness.

Hospital: a gift of healing/anointing or caring or love; edifying others.

Hotel: a place of gathering; a temporary place of meeting; a transit place of meeting; church; a transit situation.

House: one's spiritual and emotion house; personality; church.

Husband: the actual husband; Jesus Christ; (if ex-husband) a previous head over you, or something that had control over you in the past.

Incense: prayer; worship; praise; acceptable unto God.

Iron: a person or object of strength, powerful; strict rules; powerful strongholds.

Ironing: the process of correction by instructions; teaching; to talk matters over; working out problem relationships; turning from sin.

Island: something related to the island; what the island is known for, or its name.

Israel: the nation of Israel; the Christian community; the redeemed ones; authority that comes from God over men; the people of God.

Jerusalem: the establishment of peace; chosen place by God; the City of God.

Jewelry: valuable possessions; God's people; gifted person who has received abilities from the Lord; a valued object or person.

Judge: Father God; authority; anointed to make decisions; Jesus Christ.

Key: the authority to something; claim to ownership; prophetic authority; kingdom authority.

Kiss: coming into agreement; covenant; seductive process; enticement; deception or betrayal; betrayal from a trusted friend or brother/sister in Christ.

Kitchen: a place of preparing spiritual food; hunger for the Word of God.

Kneeling: surrender; praying; art of submission.

Knees: reverence; prayerfulness; submission.

Knives (or Sword): the Word of God; speaking against someone.

Ladder: changing spiritual position; escaping from captivity.

Lamb/Sheep: Jesus; believer; gentleness; blamelessness.

Lame: shortcomings; a flaw in one's walk with God; a limitation.

Lamp: a source of light; an inward part of man or spirit; the Holy Spirit.

Land: inheritance; promise given by God.

Bare earth or dust: curse; bareness.

Neglected, unwanted land: neglected promise or inheritance.

Newly cleared land: newly revealed area of God's promise.

Ripe on the land: fruitful work of the ministry.

Laugh: rejoicing; joy; sarcasm.

Laughing: an outburst of excitement or joy.

Lava: enemy.

Lawyer: Jesus Christ; mediator; the accuser of brethren; pertaining to legalism.

Lead (metal): heavy burden; heavy object.

Leaven: sin that spreads to others; false belief system.

Leaves: trees with healthy leaves planted by the rivers of life; healing of the nation; (if dry leaves) the pressures of life.

Left: that which is of the Spirit; God manifested through the flesh of man.

Legs: means of support; spiritual strength to walk in life; (if female legs) the power to entice.

Library: a place of knowledge; schooling; wisdom.

Lice: accusation; shame; a concerted attempt to smear you; (if lice on head) an excessive compulsion to lie.

Light: illumination on the established truth; no longer hidden; to show forth.

Absence of light: lack of understanding; absence of God.

Dim light: showing a need for fullness of knowledge of the Word.

Small lamp or flashlight: walking in partial founding of the Word.

Lightning: God's voice; the Lord interrupting an activity to get man's attention; something happening very quickly.

Lion: the conquering nature of Jesus; a powerful spirit, good or bad.

Lips: Word of God; offering; enticement; a means of testifying; speaking falsehood or accusation.

Living Room: part of your personality opened for others to see.

Lost (direction): indicating inner confusion or indecision.

K
L

Machines: power and mechanism of the spirit.

Man (unknown): a spiritual messenger, either God's messenger or evil; Jesus.

Manna: God's miraculous provision; coming directly from God; glory of God; bread of life.

Map: Word of God; instruction; direction.

Marble: beauty; majesty of God.

Mark: something that distinguishes; symbol; to set apart; mark of God or devil.

Marriage: going deeper into things of God (intimacy); a covenant process; an actual marriage; Jesus Christ's union with the Church.

Meat: strong doctrine; something meant for spiritually mature people.

Microphone: amplification of the Word of God; preaching; the prophetic ministry; an ability to influence many people.

Microscope: a need to look more carefully; obtaining clearer vision; to magnify a situation or circumstance, whether good or bad.

Microwave Oven: may indicate lack of patience; looking for an easy option; quick acting process.

Middle/Junior High: medium level equipping by God.

Milk: good nourishment; elementary teaching.

Mirror: something that enables you to look more closely; reflecting on a situation or circumstance; the Word of God revealing a need for change; self-consciousness; vanity.

Miscarriage: plans aborted; to lose something at the preparatory stage, whether good or bad.

Money: God's favor; spiritual and natural wealth; spiritual authority; power; man's strength; greed.

Morning: the beginning of something; the light of God after a dark season of life; sins being revealed; rejoicing.

Mother: the Church; Jerusalem; one's actual mother; a spiritual mother; caregiver/teacher.

Mother-in-law: a church that is not your actual church; false teacher; one's actual mother-in-law.

Motor (engine or battery): a source of power and anointing.

Mountain: great power and strength, whether good or bad; a place of revelation or meeting with God and His glory; obstacle; difficulty.

Mouth: an instrument of witnessing, good or bad; speaking evil or good words; something from which come the issues of life; words coming against you.

Moving: a change in spiritual and emotional well-being; a changing situation; imminent change.

Music: praise and worship; flowing in spiritual gifts; teaching; admonishing; a message.

M

Mustard Seed: faith; value or power of faith; sowing in faith; the Word of God; God's promise.

Nails: to make something more permanent; how Jesus dealt with our sins.

Name: meaning of the name; the identity of something; designate; rank or status.

Nation: could represent characteristics of the nation; a calling related to the nation; the actual nation itself.

Neck: stubborn; strong willed; (if stiff-necked) rebellious.

Nest: security that is not real; God as a place of rest.

Net: to trap or ensnare; the plans of the enemy; to win souls.

New: new condition.

Newspaper: proclamation; prophetic utterance; bringing something to the public.

Night: time of trial or difficulty; lack of God's light or understanding; without involvement of the Spirit.

Noise: irritation that is intrusive; sound that draws attention.

North: refers to great powers that will come.

Nose: discerning spirit; intruding into people's privacy; discernment, whether good or bad; one who gossips.

Nosebleed: strife; a need to strengthen your discernment.

Ocean: masses of people.

Oil: the anointing; medicine; joy; prosperity; the Holy Spirit; grace and mercy of God.

Old: old ways.

Old Man: pre-Christian self; spirit of wisdom.

Orange: warning; danger ahead; caution needed.

Oven: the heart of the matter; of high intensity; fervency.

Park: a place of rest, worship, tranquility; a temporary place.

Path: the path of life; a personal walk with God; directions in life.

Pearl: an object or person of value; an established truth of God; the glory of Heaven.

Pen/Pencil: pertaining to writing; words that are written; to make permanent.

Perfume: an aroma; the glory of God; fragrance of the Holy Spirit; anointing.

Picture: something relating to images; to keep in memory; to honor.

Frames: mindset; mentality.

Golden frames: divine seal.

Old frame: out-dated.

Pig: an unclean spirit; spirit of religion; caged by one's mindset; phony and not trustworthy; selfish; hypocritical.

Pillar: a main support, whether spiritual and natural; foundational truths.

Pit: enticement; trap; a hole on the pathway.

M
N
O
P

Platter: something on which to present things.

Play: life competition; spiritual warfare/contention.

Playing: reflective of a true-life situation; the game of life.

Plow: preparing the heart to receive the Word of God; cracking fallow grounds hardened by sin.

Poison: evil and deadly teaching or doctrine.

Police: spiritual authority; having power to enforce purpose, whether good or bad; pastor or elders; angels or demons; enforcer of a curse of the law.

Porch: exhibition; public part of a building; easily seen and openly displayed.

Postage Stamp: the seal of authority; authorization; empowered.

Pregnancy: in the process of reproducing; preparatory stage; the promise of God; the Word of God as seed; a prophetic word; process of birthing, whether good or bad.
Labor pains: final stages of trial or preparation; wilderness period.

Preacher/Pastor (Priest and Prophet): a person who represents God; a timely message from God; spiritual authority.

Prison: lost souls; bondage; areas of stronghold.

Purple: related to royalty; kingly anointing or authority.

Purse (or wallet): treasure; heart; personal identity; precious and valuable; (if empty) bankrupt.

Railroad Track: tradition; unchanging habit; stubborn; caution; danger.

Rain: blessings; God's Word; outpouring of the Spirit; hindrance; trial or disappointment.
No rain/drought: lack of blessing; absence of God's presence.

Rainbow: a sign of God's covenant; a sign of natural agreement.

Red: passion; the Blood of Jesus; strong feeling; danger; anger.

Reed: weakness, whether spiritual or natural; too weak to be relied on.

Refrigerator: heart issues; motivation; thoughts; storing up spiritual food for the right time.
Spoiled food: to harbor a grudge; unclean thoughts or desires.
Stored food: matters stored in the heart.

Refuge: a place of protection, safety or security.

Reins: a means of control or restraint.

Rending: repentance; disagreement; to tear apart as a sign of anger; grief or sorrow.

Rest: a state of stillness or inactivity; tranquility; a place where you can receive from God; laziness.

Restaurant: a place of choice regarding the spiritual food you need; a place where the five-fold ministry is taught.

P
Q
R

Resting: not in activity.

Right: authority or power; natural inclination; what you can do naturally.

Right turn: natural change.

Ring: never-ending, unchanging and uninterrupted; unity of purpose in a place; covenant relationship; relating to God's authority; symbol of our covenant with God.

Engagement ring: promise; sign of commitment.

Rings as jewelry: vanity; worldliness.

Wedding ring: marriage between man and woman.

River: movement of God; flow of the Spirit; obstacle; trial.

Deep: deep things of God.

Dangerous currents: difficulty in moving in the flow of the Spirit.

Dried up: danger ahead; lack of God's presence; traditions or legalism; empty of spiritual power.

Muddy: operating in mixtures, flesh and spirit.

Robe: righteousness; the true covering from God; right standing with God.

Rock: Jesus Christ; solid foundation; a place of refuge; an obstacle; a stumbling block.

Rocket: a ministry or person with great power or potential for deep things of the Spirit; capable of quick take-off and great speed.

Rocking: reflective.

Rocking chair: intercession; recollection; prayer; relaxation; long standing in nature; old age.

Rod: staff or scepter of authority; to guard; discipline.

Roller Coaster: needing more faith; swings of seasons or moods; a situation or circumstance that moves up and down.

Roller Skates: a skillful walk with God; speedy progress; fast, but possibly dangerous.

Roof: covering; revelation from above; zone of mind; thinking; meditation; spiritual rather than natural.

Root: motives; the origin and source; the heart of a matter, whether good or bad.

Rope/Cord: in covenant; in binding; used to bind.

Round (shape): never-ending; favor, love, or mercy.

Rowboat: a ministry that intervenes for others; offering earnest prayers.

Sacrifice: to give up something; to lay down one's life for another; something to cover up or wash away.

Salt: something that adds value, preserves, or purifies; to make lasting.

Salt Water: to add flavor; to cleanse.

Sanctuary: a sacred place; a refuge; a place of immunity or rest; a place set apart for spiritual offering and sacrifices.

Sand: numerous; seeds; promises; symbolic of a work of flesh; not suitable for a foundation.

R
S

Scepter: office (of ministry); a staff of authority or sovereignty.

School: training period; a place of teaching; a teaching ministry; anointing.

Scorpion: an evil spirit; poisonous.

Sea: great multitude of people; nations of the world; unsettled as the mark of sea; something by which to reach the nations; a great obstacle.

Seat: the power base; rulership; authority; coming to rest; a place of mercy.

Seed: the Word of God; a promise; a person or situation capable of giving rise to many or greater things, whether good or bad.

Serpent: a symbol of satan; kingdom of the world; an accursed thing; an emblem of Christ on the Cross; cunning; gossip; persecution; spirit of divination.

Sewage: something that carries away waste; a good appearance but carrying waste within; waste that could defile flesh.

Sewing: putting together; amendment; union; counseling.

Sexual Encounter: soulish desires; or want to be intimate with other person's gifts; (if with an old lover) a desire for former life.

Shadow: a reflection of a person or situation; the spiritual cover; a place of safety, security; only partially illuminated; a poor resemblance of something else; delusion or imitation; imperfect or lacking real substance; demons.

Shepherd: Jesus Christ or God; a leader, either good or bad; an ability to separate goat from sheep; a selfless person.

Shield: a protective substance; God's truth; faith in God.

Ship: a big ministry capable of influencing large numbers of people.

Battleship: built for effective spiritual warfare.

Crashing: end of ministry, or end of one phase.

Fast: operating in great power.

Large: large area of influence.

On dry ground: without a move of the Spirit; moving in works of the flesh.

Sinking: out of line with God's purpose; losing spiritual control.

Small: small or personal.

Shoes: readiness to spread the gospel; knowledge of the Word of God.

Boots: equipped for spiritual warfare.

Does not fit: walking in what you are not called for.

Giving away shoes: depending on its context, equipping others.

High heels: seduction or discomfort.

In need of shoes: not dwelling on God's Word; in need of comfort or protection.

New shoes: getting new understanding of the gospel; a fresh mandate from God.

Putting on slippers: preparation for a journey.

Snowshoes: too comfortable.

Taking off shoes: faith; walking in the spirit; supported by faith in the Word of God.

Taking someone else's shoes off: honoring God; ministering to the Lord; to show respect.

Tennis shoes: spiritual giftedness; running the race of life.

Shoulder: responsibility; authority.

Bare female shoulders: enticement.

Broad shoulders: capable of handling much responsibility.

Drooped shoulders: defeated attitude; overworked, overtired, and burned out.

Shovel: digging up something; to smear someone.

Sickle: reaping; the Word of God; a harvest.

Sieve: to separate impure from the pure; trial or testing.

Sign: a witness of something; to foreshadow; to draw attention to a person, place, or circumstance.

Crossroads/Intersection: a place for decision; a time for change.

Stop sign: to stop and pray for guidance.

Yield: a sign of submission.

Signature: commitment and ownership.

Silver: a symbol of redemption; understanding; knowledge; an object or person of valor; worldly knowledge; betrayal; a furnace of affliction.

Singing: the words of the song, equals a message from God; rejoicing; heart overflow.

Sister: one's actual sister, or her similar qualities in you or someone else; a sister in Jesus Christ.

Sister-in-law: the same as sister; one's actual sister-in-law, or a person with similar qualities; a Christian in another fellowship; a relationship without much depth.

Sitting: a place of authority; position in power; throne of God; seat of satan.

Skiing: stepping out in faith; the power of faith; smooth riding in God's provision; making rapid process.

Skins: a covering.

Sky: above the natural; God's presence; related to God or high things of the Spirit.

Skyscraper: revelation; a ministry or person with a built-up structure to function on a multilevel; a church or person with prophetic giftedness; a high level of spiritual experience.

Sleeping: being overtaken; not being conscious; hidden; laziness; state of rest; danger; out of control; (if overslept) in danger of missing a divine appointment.

Smile: a sign of friendliness; an act of kindness; agreement.

Smiling: a sign of friendship; a seductive process.

S

217

Smoke: praise; worship; the manifested glory of God; prayers of saints; hindrance.

Snake: backbiting; divination; false accusations; false prophecies; gossip; long tales; slander.

Snare: a trap; the fear of man; bringing into bondage.

Snow: favor of God; totally pure; (if dirty snow) no longer pure.

Soap: to make clean; forgiveness; interceding for others.

Socks: reflective of the state of one's heart as fertile ground for God's Word; peace; protection of the feet.

Dirty or torn socks: blemished heart and walk before God.

White socks: unblemished heart and walk before God.

Soldier: spiritual warfare; a call for more prayers, fasting, and worship; a period of trial or persecution.

Son: a child of God; a ministry or gifting from God; one's actual son, or someone with similar traits.

Sour: corrupted; false.

Spear: words, whether good or bad; the Word of God; evil words; curses.

Spider: an evil spirit that works by entrapping people; false doctrine.

Spot: a fault; contamination; (if without spot) a glorious church.

Sprinkling: spiritual change by washing away dirt; cleansing; purifying; consecrating.

Square: tradition; mindset; worldly and blind to the truth.

Stadium: tremendous impact.

Staff: a symbol or part of authority.

Stairs: means of bringing about changes.

Downstairs: demotion; backslide; failure.

Guardrail: safety; precaution; warning to be careful.

Standing: firmness in faith; committed to the belief; not finished; (if standing straight) no crookedness, but in the correct direction.

Stars: important personality; a great number; descendant; supernatural; Jesus Christ; (if falling star) apostate church.

Storm: trial; testing period; satanic attacks.

White storm: God's power; revival.

Straight: to be fixed in attitude; no ambiguity; going in the right direction.

Stumbling: to make mistakes; to fail; to be in error; lack of the truth.

Suicide: an act of self-destruction; foolishness; sinful behavior; pride; lack of hope.

Suitcase: on the move; transition; a private walk with God.

Summer: a time of harvest; an opportune time; fruits of the spirit.

Sun: the light of God; the truth; the glory of God.

S

Supper: the body and blood of Jesus; marriage supper; God's provision; God's enabling power.

Sweating: signs of intense work of the flesh; much work without Holy Spirit; a difficult and agonizing time.

Sweeping: getting rid of sinful things; cleaning a place from evil; the process of making clean; correcting process; repentance.

Sweet: something gratifying; reflecting on the Word of God; communion with the Spirit.

Swimming: moving in spiritual gifts; a prophetic utterance.

Swimming pool: Church; a place or provision available for moving in the Spirit; (if dirty) corrupt or apostate.

Swing: moving in the ups and downs of life.

Swinging: full flow of peace.
High swinging: overindulgence; fake, unnecessary risks.

Sword: the Word of God; a verbal response with the Bible; evil words.

Table: a place of agreement or covenant; to iron out issues; altar; community; fellowship.

Tail: the end or least of something; the last time.

Tar: covering; bitterness.

Tares: children of darkness; evil or deceptive ones; degenerates.

Tasting: to experience something, whether good or bad; trying something out; judging.

Teacher: Jesus Christ; Holy Spirit; a gift of God.

Tears: emotional sowing; mostly distress, but could represent brokenness; joy.

Teeth: wisdom; gaining understanding; to work something out.
Baby teeth: childish; without wisdom or knowledge; inexperienced.
Broken teeth: difficulty in coming to understanding.
Brushing teeth: gaining wisdom or understanding.
False teeth: full of worldly reasoning, instead of pure spiritual understanding.
Toothache: tribulation coming; heartache.

Telephone: spiritual communication, either good or evil; godly counsel.

Telescope: looking or planning for the future; making a problem appear bigger and closer.

Television: visionary revelation, prophetic dreams, or prophetic utterance.

Temple: a place of meeting with God; a place of refuge; God's habitation; the human body.

Thief: satan; deceiver; secret intruder; unexpected loss.

Thigh: strength; flesh; to entice; oath taken.

Thorns: evil disturbance; curse; gossip.

S
T

Throne: a seat of power; a place of authority; God's throne; an evil throne.

Thumb: apostolic; authority; soul power.

Thunder: God speaking; a loud signal from God; touching; warning; blessing.

Tin: something of low valor; not original, but an imitation.

Titanic: a big plan that is not going to work out.

Title/Deed: ownership seal; potential to possess something.

Tongue: powerful; spiritual language; national language; something that cannot be tamed.

Tornado: a distressing situation; great trouble; spiritual warfare.

Tower: a high spiritual thing; supernatural experience; great strength; pride, as in the Tower of Babel.

Tractor: a groundbreaking ministry; prepare the mind to receive.

Trailer: an equipping ministry; a caring service; a ministry that is migrating.

Train: a large ministry that influences lots of people; to move and send people out; a movement of God.

Tree: leader, whether good or bad; a person or organization; nations or kingdom.

Christmas tree: celebrations.

Evergreen tree: long-lasting or everlasting.

Oak tree: great strength; durable.

Olive tree: anointed of God; Israel; the Church; anointing oil.

Palm tree: a leader who is fruit producing.

Tree stump: tenacity or stubbornness; retaining hope despite circumstances; keeping roots in place.

Willow tree: indicating sadness; defeat.

Trophy: victory.

Truck: a personal ministry that brings provision.

Trumpet: a voice of the prophet; the second coming of Christ; proclaiming the good news; blessing; promise.

Tunnel: a passage; a time or place of transition; troubled or dark seasons of life.

Two story: multilevel giftedness; symbolic of flesh and spirit; multitalented church.

Upstairs: pertaining to the Spirit; Pentecost; zone of thought; great balance; spiritual realm.

Upward motion: moving onto higher spiritual matters.

Urinating: releasing pressure; compelling urge or temptation; repentance.

Van (moving van): a time or period of change, either in the natural or in the spirit.

Vapor: a temporary situation or circumstance; the presence of God; evidence of something.

T
U
V

Veil: to conceal; to hide glory or sin; to deceive; blind to the truth; a lack of understanding.

Vessel: people as instrument of use, whether for good or bad purposes; Christian believers.

Vine: Jesus Christ; Christian believers.

Vineyard: harvest; a place of planting; a heavenly kingdom.

Voice: a message from God or satan; the Word of God; godly instruction.

Walking: walking the path of life; life or living in the Spirit; progress.

Difficulty: trials or opposition; evil opposition to destiny.

Unable: hindrance to doing what you are called to do.

Wall: obstacle; barrier; defense; limitation; great hindrance; blocking the view of presenting spiritual signs.

War: spiritual warfare.

Washing: to clean.

Waters: the Holy Spirit; a move of the Spirit; nations of the world; instability.

Stagnant, muddy, or polluted: corrupted spiritual moves; sin; false doctrine.

Troubled water: healing pool; troubled mind.

Water fountain: God's Spirit welling up within man; salvation.

Water well: revival coming; a time of refreshing.

Weeds: sinful nature or acts.

Weight: a great responsibility, load, or burden.

Wheel: pertaining to life cycle; long-lasting; continuously.

Wife: one's actual wife; someone joined to you in covenant; a spirit of submission; the Church; Israel.

Wilderness: hard times; a place of trial/testing; distant from God; a place of training; a place of provision.

Wind: movement of the Spirit, is usually good, but may be evil; disappears quickly; unstable; difficult to understand.

Window: prophetic gifting; revelation knowledge; gaining insight.

Wine: Holy Spirit; communion; teaching; blessing; counterfeit spirit.

Wine Press: true doctrine.

Wineskins: the Body of Christ; the Church.

Wings: prophetic; under God's protection; period not suitable for work.

Winter: a season of unfruitfulness; a latent period.

Witch: a spirit of rebellion; non-submission; a manipulative person; a spirit of control.

Wolf: a tendency to destroy God's work; a false minister; an opportunistic person.

Woman (unknown): a messenger from God or satan; an angel or demonic spirit; a seducing spirit.

V
W

Wood: life; humanity; carnal reasoning; lust; dependence on the flesh.

Work Area: the place or time of your service.

Worm: something that eats from the inside, often secretly; not obvious on the surface; disease; filthiness.

Wrestling: to battle; to contend with; perseverance; a struggling in the spirit or real life.

Yoke: enslaved; bondage; tied to something, usually evil but sometimes good.

Zion: a place of strength and protection; leadership; God's Kingdom.

W
X
Y
Z

ABOUT THE AUTHOR

D R. JOE IBOJIE, founder and senior pastor of The Father's House, travels nationally and internationally as a Bible and prophetic teacher. He combines a unique prophetic gifting with rare insight into the mysteries of God and the ancient biblical methods of understanding dreams and visions. His ministry has blessed thousands by bringing down-to-earth clarity to the prophetic ministry. He is a popular speaker worldwide. He and his wife, Cynthia, live in Aberdeen, Scotland.

CONTACT INFORMATION

For additional copies of this book and other products from Cross House Books,
Contact: sales@crosshousebooks.co.uk.
Please visit our Website for product updates and news at
www.crosshousebooks.co.uk.

OTHER INQUIRIES

CROSS HOUSE BOOKS
Christian Book Publishers
245 Midstocket Road
Aberdeen, AB15 5PH, UK
info@crosshousebooks.co.uk
publisher@crosshousebooks.co.uk
"The entrance of Your Word brings light."

MINISTRY INFORMATION

DR. JOE IBOJIE IS THE SENIOR PASTOR OF
THE FATHER'S HOUSE

A family church and a vibrant community of Christians located in Aberdeen Scotland, UK. The Father's House seeks to build a bridge of hope across generations, racial divides, and gender biases through the ministry of the Word.

You are invited to come and worship if you are in the area.

For location, please visit the church's Website:

www.the-fathers-house.org.uk

For inquiries:

info@the-fathers-house.org.uk

Call 44 1224 701343

HOW TO LIVE THE SUPERNATURAL LIFE IN THE HERE AND NOW

Are you ready to stop living an ordinary life? You were meant to live a supernatural life! God intends us to experience His power every day! In *How to Live the Supernatural Life in the Here and Now* you will learn how to bring the supernatural power of God into everyday living. Finding the proper balance for your life allows you to step into the supernatural and to move in power and authority over everything around you. Dr. Joe Ibojie, an experienced pastor and prolific writer, provides practical steps and instruction that will help you to:

- Step out of the things that hold you back in life.
- Understand that all life is spiritual.
- Experience the supernatural life that God has planned for you!
- Find balance between the natural and the spiritual.
- Release God's power to change and empower your circumstances.

Are you ready to live a life of spiritual harmony? Then you are ready to learn *How to Live the Supernatural Life in the Here and Now!*

DREAMS AND VISIONS VOLUME 1

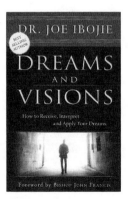

Dreams and Visions presents sound scriptural principles and practical instructions to help you understand dreams and visions. The book provides readers with the necessary understanding to approach dreams and visions by the Holy Spirit, through biblical illustrations, understanding of the meaning of dreams and prophetic symbolism, and by exploring the art of dream interpretation according to ancient methods of the Bible.

ILLUSTRATED BIBLE-BASED DICTIONARY OF DREAM SYMBOLS

This book is a companion to *Dreams & Visions: How to Receive, Interpret and Apply Your Dreams* and will help today's believers understand what dream symbols mean. When used through the Holy Spirit, it can help the reader take away the frustration of not knowing what dreams mean and avoid the dangers of misinterpretation.

—Joseph Ewen
Founder and Leader of Riverside Church Network
Banff, Scotland, UK

This book is a treasure chest, loaded down with revelation and the hidden mysteries of God that have been waiting since before the foundation of the earth to be uncovered. *Illustrated Bible-Based Dictionary of Dream Symbols* shall bless, strengthen, and guide any believer who is in search for the purpose, promise, and destiny of God for their lives.

—Bishop Ron Scott Jr.
President, Kingdom Coalition International
Hagerstown, Maryland

Illustrated Bible-Based Dictionary of Dream Symbols is much more than a book of dream symbols; it has also added richness to our reading of God's Word. Whether you use this book to assist in interpreting your dreams or as an additional resource for your study of the Word of God, you will find it a welcome companion.

—Robert and Joyce Ricciardelli
Directors, Visionary Advancement Strategies
Seattle, Washington

BIBLE-BASED DICTIONARY OF PROPHETIC SYMBOLS FOR EVERY CHRISTIAN

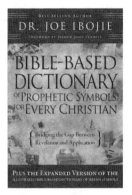

The most comprehensive, illustrated Bible-based dictionary of prophetic and dream symbols ever compiled is contained in this one authoritative book!

The Bible-Based Dictionary of Prophetic Symbols for Every Christian is a masterpiece that intelligently and understandably bridges the gap between prophetic revelation and application—PLUS it includes the expanded version of the best selling *Illustrated Bible-Based Dictionary of Dream Symbols.*

Expertly designed, researched, and Holy Spirit inspired to provide you an extensive wealth of revelation knowledge about symbols and symbolic actions, this book is divided into four parts that go way beyond listing and defining words. Rhema word and divine prompting lift off every page!

THE JUSTICE OF GOD
VICTORY IN EVERYDAY LIVING

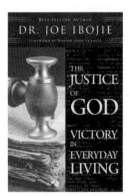

Only once in awhile does a book bring rare insight and godly illumination to a globally crucial subject. This book is one of them! A seminal work from a true practitioner, best-selling author, and leader of a vibrant church, Dr. Joe Ibojie brings clarity and a hands-on perspective to the Justice of God.

The Justice of God reveals:

- How to pull down your blessings.
- How to regain your inheritance.
- The heavenly courts of God.
- How to work with angels.
- The power and dangers of prophetic acts and drama.

THE WATCHMAN
THE MINISTRY OF THE SEER IN A LOCAL CHURCH

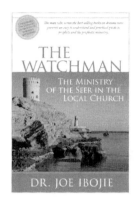

The ministry of the watchman in a local church is possibly one of the most common and yet one of the most misunderstood ministries in the Body of Christ. Over time, the majority of these gifted people have been driven into reclusive lives because of relational issues and confusion surrounding their very vital ministry in the local church.

Through the pages of *The Watchman* you will learn:

- Who these watchmen are.
- How they can be recognized, trained, appreciated, and integrated into the Body of Christ.
- About their potential and how they can be channelled as valuable resources to the local leadership.
- How to avoid prophetic and pastoral pitfalls.
- How to receive these gifted folks as the oracles of God they really are.

The 21st century watchman ministry needs a broader and clearer definition. It is time that the conservative, narrow, and restrictive perspectives of the watchman's ministry be enlarged into the reality of its great potential and value God has intended.

THE FINAL FRONTIERS
COUNTDOWN TO THE FINAL SHOWDOWN

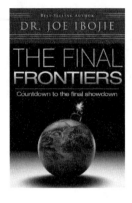

The maladies that define the focal feature of our existence are that we face a continuous threat from the challenges of the earth in a fallen state. Every now and again, we witness the eruptions of nature against man with catastrophic consequences, but these are only miniature representations of an immense cosmic cataclysm that could occur. Gradually the things that make the earth precious to us are disappearing with few taking notice. *The Final Frontiers* is a peep into the future and a call to action. It provides you with a practical approach to the changing struggles that confront humanity now and in your future and reveals through Scriptures and modern-day experiences:

- What was lost at the Fall
- The elements of nature in God's service
- How to defeat the devil at the mind game
- Invisible realms of hell
- Spiritual weaponry
- Peace and the ultimate redemption

"In writing this book, I feel like the prophet Jeremiah, calling humanity to be alert to the ploy of the enemy, to break the secret bubble, and reveal the shapes of warfare to come." —Dr. Joe Ibojie

DREAM COURSES

D REAMS ARE THE PARABLE LANGUAGE of God in a world that is spiritually distancing itself from experiencing the reality of His Presence. They are personalized, coded messages from God. Through dreams, God breaks through our thought processes, mindsets, prejudices and emotions to connect with the spirit of man. In this way He shows us what we might have missed or not heard or what our natural mind was incapable of comprehending. We all dream. He speaks to us at our individual levels and leads us further in Christ. God's ultimate purpose in dreams and visions is to align us to His plan and purposes in our lives!

The purpose of these courses is to equip the saints for the end-time move of God by learning the art of hearing Him and understanding how He speaks through dreams at an individual level.

Each dream course builds on the knowledge gained in the previous course. Attendees are strongly encouraged to take the courses in order for maximum effectiveness.

Topics covered include:

COURSE 1

- Introduction to dreams and visions.
- Biblical history of dreams and visions.
- How dreams are received.

- Hindrances to receiving and remembering your dreams.
- How to respond to your dreams.
- Differences between dreams and visions.
- Introduction to interpreting your dreams.
- Understanding the ministry of angels.

COURSE 2

- Introduction to the language of symbols (the language of the spirit).
- Different levels of interpretation of dreams.
- Why we seek the meaning of our dreams.
- What to do with dreams you do not immediately understand.
- Maintaining and developing your dream-life.
- Expanding the scope of your dreams.
- Improving your interpretative skill.
- Visions and the Third Heaven.

COURSE 3

- Responding to revelations.
- Interpreting the dreams of others.
- Guidelines for setting up a corporate dream group.
- Prophetic symbolism.
- How to organize Dream Workshops.
- The Seer's anointing.
- The ministry of a Watchman.
- Spiritual warfare (fighting the good fight).
- Understanding the roles of angels and the different categories of angelic forces.
- How to work with angels.

COURSE 4

- Living the supernatural in the natural.
- Understanding the spiritual senses.
- Maintaining balance while blending the natural and the spiritual senses.
- Security and information management in revelatory ministry.
- Understanding the anointing.
- Dialoguing with God.
- An anatomy of scriptural dreams.

WEEKEND COURSES

Friday

- Registration begins at 5:00 P.M.
- Teaching begins at 6:00 P.M.

Saturday

- Registration begins at 9:00 A.M.
- Sessions begin at 10:30 A.M., 1:30 P.M. and 7:00 P.M.

One Week Course (Monday through Friday)

Courses begin Monday morning and conclude Friday evening.

- Registration begins each day at 9:00 A.M.
- Sessions begin at 10:00 A.M. and end at 5:00 P.M.

There are breaks for lunch and tea.

The contents of each Dream Course will be covered in two weekend courses or a single one-week course (Monday through Friday).

To Request a DREAM COURSE in your area of the world,
please call to arrange a program to fit your needs:

Dr. Joe Ibojie
info@the-fathers-house.org.uk
44-1224-701343
44-7765-834253